Winning at your
I·N·T·E·R·V·I·E·W

a complete action kit

MICHAEL STEVENS

KOGAN
PAGE

First published in 1989 by
Kogan Page Ltd,
120 Pentonville Rd, London N1 9JN

Reprinted 1992

Typeset by DP Photosetting, Aylesbury, Bucks
Printed by Clays Ltd, St Ives plc

British Library Cataloguing in Publication Data

Stevens, Michael
   Winning at your interview.
   1. Job hunting. Interviews. Manuals
   I. Title
   650.1′4

   ISBN 1-85091-818-X
   ISBN 0-74940-011-9 HB

CONTENTS

HOW TO USE THIS BOOK

Interviews are inevitable in almost every career and people who can present themselves effectively at those interviews stand a better chance of success.

Most of us will be interviewed many times during our careers and the outcome can change our lives dramatically, affecting not simply our immediate prospects but our whole future. In the short term, success may mean higher pay, better prospects, perhaps more recognition; in the long term it can mean being able to choose the type of work we do and what we can achieve through that work.

Even the best qualified candidates can be unsuccessful at interviews if they do not know how to present themselves. Your performance in an interview will depend largely on how well prepared you are for it.

This book is a step-by-step guide to all that you need to do to prepare for your interview and perform well on the day. (It assumes that you have already been invited for an interview; if not, a list of books is provided at the back which should help you.)

Throughout the book there are exercises, checklists and summaries designed to help you to plan and prepare for your interview. These appear where you see the following symbols:

 Activities

for you to do, which help you to understand how interviews work and how to present yourself in the best way.

Guidelines

which help you to learn more about how to be successful at interviews.

Projects

at the end of the chapters, helping you to prepare and plan for your interview.

Key Points

to remember, as a summary of each chapter.

You will need some large sheets of paper to write notes when you are doing the Activities and Projects. Each of these has a number, which you can write at the top of your notes to help you refer to them later. The chapters are arranged to be worked through in sequence. Most of the book refers to job interviews, but you can use it in the same way to prepare for other types of interview: for a place at college or university, membership of a professional body, a bursary or grant, or promotion.

Whether you are a school-leaver facing your first job interview, or a seasoned professional wanting to improve your chances of success, this book will help to give you an edge on the competition. You will feel more relaxed and confident knowing that you can create a good impression whatever happens in the interview.

INTRODUCTION

To be successful at a selection interview requires more than having the right qualifications, knowledge and skills. People invited for an interview are usually those who have been shortlisted because they meet the basic requirements.

The purpose of selection interviews is usually to get a more complete picture of the candidates than is available from other sources, such as application forms or curricula vitae. Interviewers note such things as candidates' appearance and style of dress, their manner and personality, and their ability to express themselves. They ask questions to find out more about the candidates' aptitudes and abilities and how they have been using them in their work and leisure activities.

The successful candidate will be the one who comes across during the interview as being closest to the 'ideal' candidate – one who has all the qualities required.

It's only natural (and fair) that you may be unsuccessful at an interview when another candidate is better suited than you. But you can be unsuccessful even when you are the best candidate, simply because of the way you come across in the interview.

This was Matthew's first job interview. He felt very nervous as he walked into the interview room, but comforted himself with the thought that working as a sales assistant in an electrical shop during the past two summer holidays would count in his favour. The interview was for a trainee sales person in the hi-fi department of a large store, and he already had a good knowledge of some of the products.

After a brief chat about his journey to the interview, the interviewer explained what the job involved and then started asking questions. Matthew explained what he had enjoyed and disliked at school, and how he felt about his GCSE results, which were good. Being so nervous, he found it difficult to think of much to say. It didn't help that the interviewer kept asking him to explain a bit more; Matthew got more and more embarrassed and started mumbling his answers.

The conversation turned to his summer job and he was asked how he thought it would be different working in a large store. Matthew thought about how to answer and eventually said that hi-fi was his passion and so it would be more interesting. Other than that, he said, it would probably be very much the same.

The interviewer wanted to know how he got on with his classmates at school and whether he took part in any group activities. All Matthew could think to say was that he had made a few friends but preferred to keep to himself. He didn't play sport because he didn't enjoy the training. He did not mention that he enjoyed playing football outside school, or that he was a member of a local volunteer group – this was nothing to do with school.

The interviewer then asked how he spent his free time and Matthew took the opportunity to talk about building up his hi-fi system. After several more questions the interview ended.

Afterwards, the interviewer included these comments in her report on Matthew: 'Judging by his GCSE results, Matthew appears to have good potential for development. However, he's shy and seems to be a bit of a loner. I am doubtful that he would fit in as a member of the team.'

Like Matthew, in the example above, many people go to interviews without having thought about what will happen during their interview, particularly the sort of questions they will be asked and the impression they will create with their answers. Matthew was probably well suited for the job, but that wasn't the impression he created during the interview.

There are many reasons why people don't present themselves well during interviews. Many of the common ones can be grouped under three headings:

- lack of confidence, or nervousness;
- not knowing how interviews work and how people are selected;
- not giving the interviewer, clearly and effectively, the information needed to make a selection.

The impression you create during the interview can mean the difference between success and failure. You have to make the interviewer aware of all the reasons why you should be selected. You can only do that by preparing thoroughly for the interview.

How this book will help you

The better prepared you are for your interview, the more likely you are to be successful. This book has been designed to guide you, step by step, through all the preparation necessary to ensure that you create the best possible impression at your interview. It will help you to:

- understand how you need to prepare;
- become familiar with the way interviews are conducted;
- understand the interviewers' job and how *they* prepare for an interview;
- plan how you will prepare for your interview;
- understand how you will be assessed;
- predict what questions you will be asked;
- learn how to answer questions effectively and prepare answers to the questions you are likely to be asked;
- rehearse your interview;
- review your performance after the interview so that you can do even better next time;
- find other sources of information and advice on interviews and careers.

This book is not intended to help you to obtain a job you are not suited for – for example, by misleading the interviewer into thinking that you have skills or qualities you do not have. It requires a great deal of skill to trick an interviewer and, even if you do succeed, you will almost certainly be the loser – largely because the job will not make the best use of the skills and qualities you do have. This book will help you to present yourself in the most positive way at an interview.

1 ▶ HOW TO WIN AT YOUR INTERVIEW

Selection interviews are used in a variety of situations but their basic purpose is always the same – to help match people to a particular set of circumstances or requirements. In a job interview, for example, the interviewer will want to find out which, if any, of the people applying is best suited to taking on the job. In order to make that selection, the interviewer needs to know what the 'ideal' job holder would be like and then to assess how close each applicant comes to this ideal.

During the interview interviewers try to supplement the information they already have about candidates by asking questions, listening and observing. Interviews are also an opportunity for the candidates to ask questions – to find out more about what a job entails, for example, or the condition of employment or the prospects.

Activity 1

Before reading the guidelines below, spend at least five minutes trying to list all the reasons why people may not be successful at an interview. (Remember to head your list 'Activity 1'.)

Guidelines

People invited for interviews are generally those who meet all the basic selection criteria. The reasons for their failure at the interview are therefore mostly to do with *how they present themselves during the interview* – what they say and how they react – and how this influences the interviewer's impression of them. The closer to the ideal candidate they appear to be, the better their chances of being selected.

No one would go into an examination without knowing which subject they were being examined on, what topics and questions they could expect to arise and what type of answers are required to get a good grade. Candidates at an interview require a similar type of knowledge. They need to understand clearly:

- the purpose of the interview;
- how the interview will be conducted;
- what information the interviewer requires;
- what questions are likely to be asked;
- how best to answer these questions;
- how the successful candidate will be selected.

However confident and self-assured we may be normally, most of us feel apprehensive when going for an interview. There are many reasons for feeling nervous. For example, we may want the job desperately; we may be worried about making a fool of ourselves or appearing ignorant if we can't answer a question; or we may have been unlucky enough to have been interviewed by one of the *few* people who delight in making candidates feel uncomfortable at interviews.

Nervousness, whatever its cause, makes it very difficult to create a good impression. We may get flustered and tongue-tied, and say things that we don't really mean. No matter how good our qualifications for the job, nervousness can make us appear totally unsuitable.

Two of the basic causes of nervousness are not knowing what to expect in an interview, and concern over what sort of impression we will create. Thorough preparation for the interview – covering the areas detailed below – is one of the best ways of overcoming nervousness.

The purpose of interviews

Both the interviewer and the candidates in selection interviews have a specific purpose. The interviewer has the task of trying to find out which of the candidates is best suited to the situation. Candidates have the dual task of trying to be selected as well as ensuring that what they are applying for meets their own requirements.

Candidates must try to show during the interview how well they fit the situation. The best way to do this is to know in advance what characteristics are required in the ideal applicant. This makes it easier, through their answers to questions and their general performance, for candidates to demonstrate clearly the relevant characteristics which they possess.

Candidates must also find out, if they don't already know, whether what they are applying for suits them. If they are made an offer they will have to decide whether or not to accept. During most selection interviews you are given the opportunity to ask questions; you need to know in advance what information you may need to ask for.

How interviews are conducted

Although all selection interviews have the same basic purpose, the way they are conducted can vary. For example, it may be as short as fifteen minutes, or last an hour or more; there may be one or several interviewers present to ask you questions; you may be asked to sit some tests during the interview; and you may be required to attend a series of interviews before a final selection is made. The exact nature of your interview will be determined by factors such as the situation for which you are applying, the depth of information that is required about candidates in order to make a selection, and the normal interview procedures used by the organisation.

There are two types of selection interview in common use: the *one-to-one interview* (one interviewer talking with each applicant individually) and the *panel interview* (where each applicant talks with two or more interviewers together). Most organisations use one or other method.

Sometimes applicants will be given two or more interviews (sometimes called *sequential interviews*) before a final selection is made. An example is the so-called 'milk round', where company representatives visit colleges and universities to look for and meet potential recruits. From those candidates seen, a proportion are selected for further interviews at a later date. Sequential interviews are also more common where the successful applicant will carry heavy responsibilities. One-to-one interviews are often used to help draw up a shortlist of candidates, while either type of interview (or very occasionally both) may be used to make the final selection.

'Tests' – used to help assess candidates' abilities, aptitudes and personality – are becoming more common, but their use is not widespread. Some organisations always use them, some occasionally, some only for certain jobs, and others not at all. They are not an examination, but are simply another way of gaining accurate information about candidates to help in making a selection decision.

The length of the interview will depend on things such as the amount of time available to the interviewer, whether it is one in a series of interviews (to shortlist candidates, or to make a final selection), whether tests are being used, and whether it is a one-to-one or panel interview.

For a number of reasons it is an advantage to know as much as possible about how your interview will be conducted. The information an interviewer requires (and therefore the questions asked) in a short-listing interview, for example, will be different from that required when making a final selection. The longer the interview the deeper the interviewer can probe with questions and the more thorough you will need to be in preparing for those questions. In a panel interview, where each interviewer may concentrate on particular topics, you may be asked a broader range of questions than in a one-to-one interview.

The general atmosphere in interviews also varies. Panel interviews, for example, tend to be more formal and so it is more difficult to feel relaxed and comfortable, particularly if you were expecting the more chatty atmosphere that is common in the 'milk round' interviews held at colleges.

If you go to an interview without at least having tried to find out how it will be conducted – and how this will affect how you need to prepare – you put yourself at a disadvantage.

The information interviewers require

Since interviews are the crucial stage in making a selection, interviewers do not have an easy task. They often have to find out a lot about each candidate in a relatively short time. The exact nature of the information they require will depend on the purpose of the interview. The ideal person for the position of assistant marketing executive, for example, will have different characteristics to those required in a junior storeman. Similarly, in interviewing people for places at college, the interviewer will be looking for different things depending on whether the course is in, say, mathematics or one of the social sciences.

Interviewers do a varying amount of preparation, often depending upon their skill as an interviewer and the selection or recruitment policies of the organisation. At their most thorough, they make a list of the characteristics required in the ideal applicant and spend some time thinking about how they will find out whether candidates have these characteristics.

There are a number of ways in which interviewers obtain this information. Candidates' answers to questions are the major source, but things such as their appearance, manner and behaviour can be equally important. If you know what type of information the interviewer is looking for, and how this will be obtained, you can begin to plan how you want to present yourself.

The questions interviewers ask

When someone tells you their address you can be fairly confident about using that information to send them a letter or to find their home. However, suppose you asked whether they could lead a group of people at work, or use a word processor? If they answered yes, how confident would you be in employing one of them to do that job?

Interviewers need accurate, objective information about candidates. If they simply ask a series of questions such as 'Do you work well with other people?', or 'Can you work out a budget?', they cannot be sure that the answers they get will be an accurate reflection of the candidates' abilities. Instead, they generally ask about topics such as work experience, leisure interests and schooldays, looking for evidence of whether or not the candidates possess the qualities required.

The emphasis interviewers place on each topic, the depth of coverage, and the specific aspects they explore, largely depend on what information they require. When you know what this is, you can predict what type of questions you will be asked.

How best to answer questions

If you walked into an interview knowing exactly what the interviewer wanted to hear from the ideal candidate, and gave a convincing performance, you could be certain that you would stand a good chance of success. Once you know what questions you are likely to be asked, and what information the interviewer will be looking for in your answers, you can decide on the best way to reply. You can prepare answers which highlight the qualities you possess which make you suitable for selection.

However, answering questions well involves a number of factors other than knowing what information you want to give. Interviewers can discover quite a lot about candidates from the way that they structure their answers and speak.

Under the pressure which many of us feel in interviews, answering questions well is not always easy. The best way to overcome this problem is to prepare thoroughly, deciding what information you want to give and then practising giving your answers so that they create the best possible impression.

Selecting the successful candidate

After all the candidates have been interviewed, the information gathered about them is used to decide how they compare with the 'ideal'. Many factors are considered, not all of which necessarily relate directly to how well they could do the job. The way candidates dress (does it fit the company 'image'?), their personality (will they get on well with others?), their ambitions (will they stay long enough to make it worthwhile training them?), their expectations for the job (will they be too impatient for promotion?), and a host of other things will be taken into account. You need to consider these factors as a part of your preparation.

PLANNING FOR SUCCESS

There is a great deal that you can do before an interview to improve your chances of success.

Activity 2

Before reading the guidelines below, list all the things you would do in preparation for being interviewed for a job. (These are similar for all types of selection interview.) Your notes from Activity 1, and the Guidelines above, will help you.

Guidelines

To make the best of the opportunity which an interview presents, you need to:

- understand how interviews in general are conducted and find out how your interview will be conducted;
- understand how people are assessed;
- understand what your interviewer is trying to achieve and know broadly what information he or she requires;
- know what information you want from the interview;
- decide what qualities the ideal applicant should possess;
- decide what questions you are likely to be asked;
- prepare outline answers to these questions which show effectively the necessary qualities you possess;
- practise how you will answer questions and behave during the interview.

The remainder of this book is designed to help you to follow these steps and prepare thoroughly for your interview. Even the most thorough preparation provides no guarantee that you will be successful at an interview. However, not preparing is likely to have the same results as not attending the interview – failure. Interviews are an opportunity to change your future, and it is up to you to make the most of it.

Chapter 2 helps you to see how some of the factors mentioned in this chapter come together in an interview.

Key Points

- Interviewers try to assess how closely each candidate matches the 'ideal' person for the situation.
- They gather detailed information about each candidate by asking questions, listening, and through observation.
- To maximise your chances of success, you need to present yourself in a way which highlights the qualities you possess which match those of the ideal applicant.

Project 1

Think about the most recent job interview you have attended or, if you haven't been interviewed for a job, the most recent occasion on which you were asked questions about yourself (eg a talk with a careers adviser). Answer *yes* or *no* to the following questions:

- Did you know broadly why the interviewer asked each question?
- Were you able to give all the information the interviewer was seeking in asking each question?
- If you had the opportunity to do the interview again, would you answer all the questions in exactly the same way?
- Overall, do you think the impression you created was as good as it could have been?
- Was the outcome of the interview what you wanted?

Look at the questions to which you answered 'no'. For each one, write down how you would have needed to prepare for the interview in order to have answered 'yes'. Remember to head these notes 'Project 1'.

2 ▶ WHAT HAPPENS IN INTERVIEWS – AN EXAMPLE

It is a natural human reaction to feel nervous and apprehensive going into a situation where we are uncertain what will happen. This is particularly true of interviews because, wanting to create a good impression, we are all the more anxious to know how best to react.

This chapter contains extracts from a fictional interview designed to help you become familiar with some aspects of the interview process.

 Activity 3

Christine Twomy is being interviewed for the post of Administrative Assistant in the finance section at the head office of a large construction company. The job advertisement included the sentence, 'The post involves working in a small team and would suit a person with ambition to progress in a job requiring a degree of responsibility and mature attitude.'

Christine wants to leave her current (first) job, where she has worked for ten months, because she feels that the company is not interested in her development and advancement. She has received no training and very little guidance from the people she works with. The work involves maintaining records, including entering on to the computer details of service work carried out. The accounts department uses this information to prepare invoices.

As you read what happens during the interview, make notes about:

- how well Christine is handling the interview (list both the good and the bad points); and

- how you think she could have created a more positive impression (what could she have said or done differently?).

Use the numbers shown against Christine's answers to indicate which parts of the interview you are writing about.

(The interviewer has just finished explaining what the job entails and giving some background information about the company.)

Interviewer   Tell me a bit about yourself, Christine.

(Christine thinks for a few seconds before she speaks and, as she answers, sometimes pauses for a long time before continuing.)

Christine (1)   Ummm ... I'm 18. I went to Gray's Comprehensive and left about 18 months ago ... then I got a job with Williamson's, where I'm working now. ... I live at home with my parents at the moment. ... I did maths and sciences at school, and one of my main interests is computers. Ummm ... I work in the service department, keeping records of all the service calls ...

(When Christine stops speaking, the interviewer looks at her and waits a little while before asking some questions about school, including what she had enjoyed, what she disliked, and whether she took part in any extra-curricular activities. They talk for a couple of minutes about what she did as a member of the school's computer club.)

Interviewer   Why do you want to leave your job at Williamson's?

Christine (2)   I don't enjoy it, really.

Interviewer   What do you dislike about it?

Christine (3)   Nothing especially. It's just not the sort of job I want.

(The interviewer watches Christine carefully as he asks the next question.)

Interviewer   Do you have any problems with the work?

Christine (4)   ... No, it's quite interesting. I enjoy it.

Interviewer   How do you get on with the people you work with?

(Christine hesitates for several seconds and then answers in a quiet voice, avoiding looking at the interviewer.)

Christine (5)   They're ok.

(The interviewer pauses to write something down.)

Interviewer   What do your parents think about you leaving the job?

Christine (6)   I've discussed it with them and they agree ... they understand my reasons.

Interviewer	I see. How do you think you would enjoy working with a small team of people, most of whom are much older than you?
Christine (7)	I don't mind really. I'm sure it would be fine.
Interviewer	Mmmm. You would be very busy. How do you think you would cope with the pressure?
Christine (8)	I'm very organised … I think that would help. We had a major change in our record system a couple of months ago. That meant checking every record and reclassifying some of the information. It had to be done in two weeks and I quite enjoyed the challenge.

(*Christine is then asked to explain exactly what this change involved, how it affected her work, and whether that had anything to do with her wanting to leave. To the last question she replied no.*)

Interviewer	What appeals to you about this job?
Christine (9)	Ummm … it sounds interesting work and the prospects are good.
Interviewer	What would you like to be doing in five years' time?
Christine (10)	Oh, I don't really know. I suppose anything as long as it's interesting. (*Laughing slightly*) A lot could happen in five years.

(*The interviewer frowns slightly, but Christine says nothing more.*)

Interviewer	This is a responsible position because you would be processing authorisations for the payment of expenses. It requires careful attention to detail. Do you think you would be good at that?
Christine (11)	Yes, I think so.
Interviewer	Do you have any experience of preparing reports?
Christine (12)	Well, I have to collect details of all the information that I process each month, for the manager. That covers things like response times to service calls, duration of the service visit, and cost.
Interviewer	Oh good. Is there anything you would like to avoid in a job?
Christine (13)	(*Answering without time to think.*) No.
Interviewer	Do you think you would enjoy working for us?
Christine (14)	Yes, I'm sure I would.
Interviewer	If we were to offer you the job, we would have to ask Williamson's for a reference. You don't have any objections to that?
Christine (15)	(*Looking surprised and a bit worried.*) No.
Interviewer	OK, Christine, I think that's all I need to know. Is there anything you would like to ask me?
Christine (16)	Umm. (*She pauses to think*) No, I can't think of anything.

(*The interviewer then thanks Christine for coming and shows her out.*)

Before going on, re-read the whole of this dialogue to see if you want to make any further comments.

Guidelines

You may have noted more points than are covered here, which are only the most important ones. Compare them with what you have written.

1. Christine has trouble thinking of what to say about herself. The interviewer probably had most of this information on her application form. The question was probably intended to find out how well she could explain herself and order her thoughts, and to gain an idea of what type of person she was from the things that were uppermost in her mind.

   Christine's repeated pauses between comments could give the impression that she is not a very quick thinker, although the real reason is that she's very nervous. Because her comments jump between school and work and back again, it gives the impression that she doesn't think very clearly. The interviewer paused and seemed to expect her to say more. She could have predicted being asked this question and decided in advance what she would like to say.

2-5. The interviewer tried repeatedly to find out why Christine wants to leave her job at Williamson's. The reason – that she is not getting any support from the company or her colleagues to advance in her work – would have been perfectly acceptable if she had explained it. In fact, since the interviewer was looking for someone with ambition, it could have been in her favour.

3. Christine misleads the interviewer by saying, 'It's not the sort of job I want.'

4. When the interviewer asked if she has any problems with the work, Christine should have realised that it was essential to explain the situation.

5. The interviewer then suspects that Christine does not get on with the people she works with. When she says, 'They're OK', in a quiet voice and avoids looking at the interviewer, it tells him that this is a problem. Without any explanation from Christine, he probably assumed that either she didn't like them or she was difficult to work with, or both.

6. By saying that she has talked to her parents about leaving her job, the interviewer gains the impression that she has given this careful thought. It suggests a mature attitude – which is one of the qualities required for the job.

7. The interviewer is still concerned about Christine's ability to work with other people. She misses another opportunity to explain the situation at Williamson's, and gives an unconvincing answer which probably confirms the interviewer's earlier impression.

8. Christine is showing, by explaining her relevant experience, that she can cope with a heavy workload. Mentioning that she is very organised also gives the interviewer more information about her skills, which could be relevant to the need for accuracy in the job.

9. Christine would have sounded more interested in the job if she had explained more about what aspects of it interested her.

10. After her previous answer, this makes it sound as if Christine has little ambition, no career plans, and is just going to let fate take its course (which is not true). This is emphasised by the laugh she gives when she says, 'A lot could happen in five years.' Even when the interviewer frowns, showing either surprise, concern or disapproval, she does not try to alter the impression she has given.

11. Christine missed this opportunity to mention her experience which is relevant to the job. Instead of replying, 'Yes, I think so', she could have said something like, 'Yes, I am sure I would. It is something I do in my current job. The records I keep are used for charging service work to customers and so I have to be very careful that there are no mistakes.'

12. This is a good example of how Christine could show, by explaining her relevant experience, that she has the knowledge and skills required for the job.

13. Christine didn't give this question any thought, perhaps because she was worried that anything negative she said could harm her chances of getting the job. However, the interviewer would have realised that she hadn't thought before answering. This quality is not compatible with attention to detail, or a sign of maturity – both qualities required in the job.

14. This was another missed opportunity for Christine to say why this job appeals to her.

15. Christine's look of surprise and worry when the interviewer mentioned a reference probably reinforced his impression that she had a problem at Williamson's.

16. This was a final opportunity for Christine to show that she was very interested in the job. She could have asked now about the opportunities for advancement and what training would be provided. This would have gone some way to rectifying her apparent lack of ambition and commitment to the job shown earlier in the interview.

These are only a selection of the ways in which interviewers can gather information about candidates, but they show how, with some preparation, you can make a more positive impression. The remaining chapters of this book are devoted to helping you do that preparation for your interview.

Key Points

- The more you know about what is going to happen in your interview, the more relaxed and confident you are likely to feel.
- It is important to understand how the interviewer may interpret what you say and do, and so gain an impression of you.
- Preparation helps you to decide in advance how to create the best possible impression.

Project 2

List the things which Christine's example suggests that you should do in preparation for a job interview. When you have done this, look at your notes from Activity 2 and Project 1 to see if there is anything in those that you should add to this list.

3 ▶ THE INTERVIEWER'S JOB

It is important to remember that interviewers are only doing a job. When you understand what this job involves, and what your interviewer is trying to achieve, it is easier for you to prepare for your interview. This chapter helps you to look at your interview from the interviewer's point of view.

Who does the interviewing?

Which person is chosen to interview candidates usually depends on the organisation and the type of job involved. Most large companies and some smaller ones have a personnel department, or an individual responsible for personnel, whose job may include interviewing potential recruits. Alternatively, the manager who will be responsible for the work of the new recruit may conduct the interviews.

In larger organisations candidates may be interviewed by both a personnel representative and their potential manager. At panel and sequential interviews each of the interviewers may represent a different department or role within the organisation. Sometimes there may also be other people involved, such as 'headhunters' or other staff-recruitment agencies (employed by the organisation to find potential recruits) and psychologists (employed to help assess candidates).

Selection interviews other than for jobs are generally conducted by a person with that particular responsibility. Interviews for places at college, for example, will often be conducted by the head of the relevant department.

It is an advantage to know what job the person interviewing you does because it will help you to understand what they might be looking for in the ideal candidate. Although, overall, this will be the same whoever conducts the interviews, different interviewers may place varying emphasis on the value of the characteristics which are being sought. A personnel officer, for example, may be particularly interested in how candidates would fit into the organisation and whether they will stay long enough to make it worthwhile investing in their training; other managers may feel it is more important to know how well candidates would fit into their team and how they could contribute immediately to its work.

Activity 4

Before reading the guidelines, describe what you think an interviewer needs to do in order to find the 'right' person for a particular job.

Guidelines

An interviewer's primary task is to select the candidate best suited for the situation in question. In job interviews this involves selecting the person who will achieve the results required from a particular job function.

Interviewers differ in the way that they view their task and the importance they give to it, but the selection of new recruits is one of the most important functions in any organisation. Mistakes can be costly in terms of the recruitment costs, lost output, and the effect that the wrong person in a job can have on other workers. Today's recruits determine the success or failure of tomorrow's organisation.

Because of the importance of selection and recruitment, nearly all large organisations and many smaller ones use a set procedure for the purpose. Although the person who conducts the interviews may not be involved at all stages of this process, it is important for you to understand the basic stages involved. Even if the organisation to which you are applying does not use such a procedure (and you may never know whether they do or not), it will help you to prepare more thoroughly for your interview.

The selection procedure might typically involve the following stages:

- compiling a job specification or job description;
- compiling a personal profile of the ideal candidate;
- attracting applicants;

- shortlisting;
- planning the interview;
- interviewing;
- selection.

In many organisations these stages will not be defined in a formal selection procedure, and a varying amount of effort and detail will be put into the process. All types of selection interview will be a part of a similar process, whether or not it is well defined and carried out rigorously.

Job specifications

In order to select someone who will be suitable for a particular job (or any specific situation) it is vital, first, to know a great deal about that job (or situation). This information – in the form of a *job specification* (or job description) – varies enormously, but may include the following:

- job title;
- location of the work;
- the job function within the organisation;
- who will be responsible for the job holder;
- brief details of the main duties of the job holder, including tasks, their purpose, and the results required;
- specific responsibilities – for completion of work, for staff, materials, budgets, etc;
- who the job holder will work with;
- terms and conditions, such as hours, pay, shifts, leave, bonuses;
- the training provided;
- career prospects of the job holder within the organisation.

In some situations it is difficult to create a precise job specification. Trainees recruited by many large organisations, for example, are moved through a variety of jobs as part of their training. The skills and knowledge this type of recruit will require in the future are impossible to predict. The job specification is therefore more likely to specify that the successful applicant shows potential for development through on-the-job experience and training.

Although not all interviewers will have a job specification, it is very useful in deciding what type of person would be best suited to a particular job. An example is given in Figure 1.

Job Title Customer Services Assistant

Location Baring House, head office.

Department Customer Services.

Job function Customer liaison – product complaints, warranty claims and service calls

Main Duties

Deal with incoming correspondence and telephone calls.
Locate purchase and service records on VDU.
Check and process complaints, claims and service calls.
Notify local Service Centres.
Maintain computer records.
Prepare monthly analysis of customer contact.

Key responsibilities

Speedy resolution of all customer problems.
Maintain accurate and up-to-date records.

Department Supervisor, 4 Assistants.

Responsible to Customer Services Supervisor.

Hours 9.00 am – 5.30 pm.

Terms £7,575 – £8,901; 26 days' paid leave.

Benefits Non-contributory pension scheme; season ticket loan; subsidised staff restaurant; sports and recreational facilities.

Training &
Development On-the-job training; potential to transfer to management trainee programme.

Figure 1 *Example of a job description*

Personal profiles

A personal profile gives details of the abilities, qualities and experience that the person requires in order to do the job effectively, including factors such as an ability to fit into the existing team of workers. Other characteristics may also be specified. For example, candidates may be required to have a manner and appearance, or a particular attitude or philosophy about the profession or industry, in keeping with that of the organisation. Today, when great care is taken by organisations to project the right image, this type of factor is becoming increasingly important.

A personal profile can take a variety of forms, but generally it classifies the characteristics required under a number of headings. The headings that are used vary considerably, but taken together they cover the same type of information. Those given below are just one way of classifying the information, but they illustrate how interviewers can use them to translate the job specification into a list of characteristics required in the ideal applicant.

Knowledge, skills and experience

What does the person have to know and be able to do in order to carry out this work? What type of general experience would equip someone for the job? Is any specific experience required? Are certain formal qualifications needed? Is a certain minimum level and standard of education required? Are any special abilities or aptitudes required, for example, driving skills, manual dexterity?

Intellectual factors

Will the job holder require above-average intelligence? What type of thinking does the job call for – analytical, creative? What particular intellectual demands does the job make – solving complex problems, negotiating, the ability to learn quickly, or to think under pressure? What particular aptitudes are required? Are there any factors which would make someone unsuitable for the job or unable to do it?

Personality

How is the job holder required to behave with people in general, and with specific groups or individuals? What type of attitudes are required – to work, colleagues, the organisation? Will certain personal qualities be required, such as patience, the ability to work under pressure? What type of manner is required – decisive, confident, persuasive?

Motivation

What does the job holder need to enjoy doing? Is there anything the job holder must not dislike? Is there anything unpleasant involved in the job? Is a certain level of commitment required? Are any special qualities required, like persistence, determination, competitiveness? Are any particular ambitions required? Does the job require a particular level of effort or energy?

Physical qualities

Are any specific physical qualities required – strength, height, good colour vision? Does the job require a particular physique or level of stamina? Is a certain physical appearance required?

Disposition

Does the job call for a certain manner or style of behaviour – authoritative, courteous, independent? Is there any characteristic which would make a person unsuitable, such as being gullible or argumentative? Does the job require a specific level of grooming or dress sense?

Circumstances

Does the job involve unsocial hours? Are the hours long? Does the job involve relocation, or extensive travel? Does the job holder require own transport? Is there anything unusual about the job which could conflict with the average person's personal circumstances?

These are just some of the areas that may be covered. There is considerable overlap between the categories, but together they enable a detailed profile to be created.

It would be unusual to find a candidate who matched the personal profile exactly, and so the characteristics required are sometimes classified as being either essential or just desirable. A measure may also be put on certain characteristics, for example, at least six months' general clerical experience may be required.

The personal profile can include characteristics which should be avoided in the candidate. For example, in selecting a person who will have to cope with difficult situations, it would be wise to avoid candidates who get flustered easily or cannot think under pressure. An example of a personal profile is given in Figure 2.

Profiles like these are *not used* by the majority of interviewers, although organisations such as the Civil Service and some large companies use them. When they *are* used the interview is likely to be more thorough and follow a more consistent line of questioning. However, most interviewers will be less well prepared and less methodical in their questioning.

It doesn't matter whether your interviewer is using this type of approach or not, provided that you prepare thoroughly for your interview. Most interviewers will be seeking the same type of information and later you will see how you can use this method of preparation to help you predict the type of questions you are likely to be asked.

Attracting applicants

In addition to the people who write to an organisation on the chance that they may have a vacancy, there are a number of ways in which organisations can attract applicants. These include advertisements in the national and local press, professional and other specialist journals, local radio, notices displayed within the organisation (on notice boards and in house journals), staff recruitment agencies, and by word of mouth. The amount of information given about a job, the way it is worded, and the prominence of the advertisement, varies depending on the medium that is used and the organisation. Competition for good recruits has always been high and is continuing to grow. In order to attract people who are likely to have the right characteristics for the job, but not to discourage those who may be doubtful about their suitability, advertisements often give only a brief outline of what the job entails, or make it sound more attractive than it is. Further information about the job is often sent to applicants along with the official application form. You will see later how you can use information from both these sources to help you to prepare for your interview.

Shortlisting

It is common for large organisations to receive many hundreds of applications in response to a job advertisement. It would be too costly and time-consuming to interview such a large number of people, even if they appeared to have many of the qualities required. Usually only a select number are invited for interview. This shortlist is created by comparing the details available about each applicant with the qualities required in the ideal candidate. This information may come from a variety of sources such as application forms and curricula vitae, and Biodata questionnaires (although these are not widely used) which help

Job Title: Housing Assistant, Housing Advice Centre.

Knowledge, Skills and Experience:
Educated to 'O'-level or equivalent.
1–2 years' clerical experience.
Good communication skills – written and oral.
Good telephone skills.
Familiarity with computer database systems.
Able to type 40 wpm.

Intellectual factors:
Able to learn quickly.
Shows initiative.
Can identify with the homeless and disadvantaged.
Able to work in a systematic way.

Personality:
Pleasant and outgoing.
Able to work as part of a team.
Calm under pressure.
Able to adapt.
Enthusiastic.

Motivation:
Good attendance record.
Conscientious.
Self-starter.
Enjoys meeting people.
Persistence in resolving problems.
Commitment to helping the homeless.

Physical qualities:
Good health.
Tidy appearance.

Disposition:
Helpful and friendly.
Sympathetic and caring.
Tactful.
Sense of humour.

Circumstances:
Able to work one Saturday morning in three, and until 7.00 pm two days a week.

Figure 2 *Example of a personal profile*

to identify the skills, qualifications and personality factors which candidates possess relevant to the job.

If you are invited for an interview it means that, from the information available about you, the organisation feels that you may be suitable for the job.

Planning the interview

The amount of planning individual interviewers carry out before conducting interviews varies enormously. Some will spend a considerable amount of time thinking about the information they require, the type of questions they will ask, and how they will assess what candidates say. Others will do no planning at all.

Of the interviewers who do prepare, some will think about the information they need to obtain under a new set of headings. These are the topics on which they will ask candidates questions. Typically, these could be: present job, education and training, previous work history, leisure interests, and family background. Different interviewers may use different headings and they can vary according to the situation. When interviewing school leavers, for example, interviewers will ask about school rather than work, and probably also give more emphasis to leisure interests, to try and find out what the candidates are like. You can use these types of heading to help you to prepare.

Interviewing

When interviewers greet candidates they will know with varying accuracy what information they need to obtain from them to assess their suitability for the situation in question. Most of the interview is devoted to trying to draw out this information from the candidates, by asking questions, listening and through observation. Ideally, the interviewer will be trying to:

- establish the facts
- check the accuracy of the information given by candidates (eg the hobbies and experience they have stated);
- gain an impression of the type of people they are (manner and personality);
- decide, from their past experience, how they are developing (personally and in their career);

- decide whether this trend will help them to develop within the organisation;
- explore their intentions for the future;
- assess how the candidates think and express themselves;
- find out their likes and dislikes (tasks, people, situations, and so on);
- give candidates an accurate impression of the job and the organisation;
- find out whether this suits individual candidates;
- find out whether they are committed to the job and the organisation;
- make these sound appealing to candidates.

The way interviewers approach this task varies considerably. In general, the more experienced and skilled they are the more smoothly their interviews run. However, whether you are interviewed by an experienced or an inexperienced interviewer, there are always advantages and disadvantages. With an experienced interviewer the atmosphere is likely to be more relaxed and the questioning will be easier to follow, but the probing will be thorough and you will be expected to give satisfactory answers. Inexperienced interviewers may be nervous and hesitant in asking questions, perhaps not speaking clearly so that it is sometimes difficult to understand the questions. However, they probably will not probe as deeply or expect such thorough answers, so you may have better control over the information you give about yourself and more opportunity to create a positive impression.

An important part of the interviewer's task is to give candidates relevant information about the job and the organisation, and try to answer any questions they may ask. The interviewer should also try to make working for the organisation sound appealing, so that the selected candidate is more likely to accept the job offer.

Activity 5

Make a list of the problems that you think interviewers face in achieving what they set out to do in an interview.

Guidelines

As well as finding out how well each candidate could do the job in question interviewers need to identify less easily recognised characteristics, such as commitment to the job, and whether candidates can develop within the organisation and possibly take on more senior positions at a later stage in their careers. The main problems they face in obtaining this information can be summarised as:

Getting candidates to talk openly
When people feel nervous they tend to say less and be less open about themselves. Interviewers can only get a true picture of candidates if they get them to talk freely and openly.

Getting the right information
Even though interviewers may know precisely what information they require, obtaining it is not straightforward. Imagine you wanted someone to do something important for you, and you had to find out if that person had the necessary skills. Unless you are very trusting and will accept a simple answer of 'yes', you would need the person to explain their relevant experience or even demonstrate their abilities. But if that information didn't quite convince you, perhaps because their experience was not directly relevant to your situation, you would find it difficult to judge their suitability. Interviewers have the same problem, only more so. They need to obtain a wide range of personal details from candidates which is sufficiently relevant and convincing to base a decision on.

Getting at the truth
It is difficult for an interviewer to know whether a candidate is deliberately omitting information, or even lying. There are many reasons why applicants for a job may want to distort the truth. For example, they may want to conceal a period of unemployment or dismissal from a job, or they may invent interests and experience which make them appear more suitable for the job. To get a true picture of candidates the interviewer needs to distuinguish fact from fiction.

Getting a complete picture of the person
If an interviewer fails to recognise in an otherwise suitable candidate the fact that he or she is, say, untrustworthy, the selection of that candidate could be a serious mistake. The same would be true if the interviewer failed to recognise all of the positive qualities which made one candidate the best person for the job, and therefore chose another candidate. Interviewers need to obtain a complete picture of each candidate, covering all aspects which may have a bearing on their performance in the job.

Shortage of time

It takes a long time to get to know a person well and yet interviewers are expected to be able to assess candidates after a relatively brief meeting, so they need to make the best possible use of the time available.

Interviewers can overcome these problems in a number of ways. The choice of the style of interview has some influence. One of the advantages of using a panel interview is that the final selection will not depend upon one person's opinion of the candidates but upon the collective decision of all of the interviewers. The interviewers often concentrate their questions on different topics, which helps to get a more complete picture of the candidates. The major disadvantage is that candidates usually feel less at ease, and therefore are less open, when faced by perhaps four or five interviewers.

Sequential interviews have the advantage that a decision is not made based upon one meeting, but upon two or more meetings. This gives interviewers more time to obtain the information required and candidates sometimes feel more at ease, and more able to talk freely, at second or third interviews.

There are a variety of techniques that interviewers can use during an interview to help them obtain the information they require. These are examined in detail in later chapters but they include:

- making candidates feel at ease;
- the type of questions they ask and the way they phrase them;
- non-verbal prompting, such as period of silence;
- rephrasing and summarising what candidates say;
- observing candidates' reactions and behaviour;
- exercises and tests.

At the end of the interviews, the interviewer should have sufficient information about each candidate to be able to judge their suitability and make a selection.

Selection

Selection of the best candidate involves comparing the information available about each individual with the personal specification or, if there isn't one, the interviewer's image of the ideal candidate. This process is not always straightforward. For example, if two candidates have the qualities required but each is stronger in different areas, the interviewer has to decide which qualities are most important to the job and which candidate has the best mix of strengths. In addition, certain characteristics – like drive and leadership qualities – are difficult to quantify and compare.

Interviewers may also have to contend with their personal biases. It is relatively easy to let judgement be swayed unreasonably by a pleasing characteristic (such as a pleasant personality, or excellent grooming), or an irritating one (like outlandish clothes, or nail biting).

When a candidate has been selected, before an offer is made, references may be taken up. If these support the selection then the offer goes forward, possibly subject to a successful medical examination.

This chapter has given you an idea of what is involved in finding someone suitable for a particular situation. The next chapter will show you what you need to do to make the best of your opportunity in the interview.

Key Points

- Interviewers vary in the amount of preparation they do, if any, but ideally they should have a list of the characteristics required in the ideal candidate and an idea of how they will find out if the candidates have these characteristics.
- This information is detailed and includes many factors other than the skills and knowledge required to do the job.
- Interviewers can use a variety of techniques to control the interview and help to overcome the problems they face in getting a full and accurate impression of candidates.

Project 3

This is designed to help you to make a list of all the information your interviewer is likely to want to obtain during your interview.

1. Try to write a *job specification* giving details of the job for which you are applying, like the example given on page 26. (If you are going for some other type of interview, you should write a 'specification' or description of the situation for which you are applying.)

    A number of sources of information are available to help you compile this job specification. They include:

    - the job advertisement;
    - the application form;

- a job description (which may have been sent with your application form);
- other information from the organisation (eg a brochure about the company);
- your knowledge of the type of job and the organisation;
- other people's knowledge of these.

2. Now use these job details to compile a *personal specification*, like the example shown on page 30. (The job advertisement may state *some* of the qualities required.) Don't worry if you think you have left something out. You will have the opportunity to fill any gaps later, but do spend as much time as you need to make your list as complete as possible before you read on.

4 YOUR ROLE FOR THE INTERVIEW

You should now understand what interviewers are trying to achieve during an interview and how they prepare for and set about achieving that task. This chapter outlines what you need to do, both in preparation and during your interview.

Two things above all that you should aim to achieve in your interview are:

- to find out whether the job (or situation) is what you want and suits you; and
- to ensure that you present your knowledge, skills, and other characteristics which make you suitable for the situation, in the most effective way.

Thorough preparation is the best way of ensuring that you can achieve both of these objectives. Having worked through the previous chapters you should be aware of many of the things this involves, but it will make things clearer if you consider first what you need to do during the interview.

DURING THE INTERVIEW

Your performance during the interview is crucial to whether or not you are successful. You know that you are in with a chance, otherwise you would not have been invited for an interview.

Activity 6

Look at the statement of your basic objectives given above and make a list of what you need to do during the interview to achieve them.

 Guidelines

The key to achieving these two objectives is the information that you convey to, and obtain from, the interviewer. Selection interviews are a two-way process where the candidates and interviewer exchange information in order to achieve their mutual goals. You must take an active role in this process.

Is what's on offer right for you?

Usually, the easier of the two objectives to achieve is finding out whether the job (or situation) suits you and is what you want. If you are offered the job you will have to decide whether or not to accept. To make the right decision you need to know what you want – not always easy – and what the situation offers.

Only you can decide what you want. However, it is worth bearing in mind that if you accept an unsuitable situation then at the very least you will not be fully satisfying your immediate needs. At worst, it could harm the rest of your career.

Once you know what you want, you can find out whether the position is going to provide these things. Towards the end of the interview most interviewers will ask you if there is anything you want to know which has not been covered. Most of it will have been, either during the interview or in the literature you have been given, but this is your opportunity to fill in any gaps and clarify important points.

What questions you want to ask will depend on how much information you have already, on your particular interests, and on the situation for which you are applying, but they should reflect a keen interest in working for the organisation. These are just some of the topics that you may want to cover:

- the people you would be working with;
- the structure of the department;
- routine, and difficult, aspects of the work
- the full responsibilities of the job;
- the type and extent of your authority;
- whether the nature of the work is changing;

- how deeply involved you would become in the work of the department;
- support and guidance available to you;
- the amount of travel involved;
- how often your performance would be reviewed;
- the amount of contact and involvement you would have with other departments;
- training and development – opportunities, courses, on-the-job training, induction;
- promotion and career prospects and the typical career path;
- conditions of employment;
- details of the salary structure and other benefits;
- recreational activities and facilities;
- when the selection will be made.

The information you require at other types of selection interview may be very different. At a college interview, for example, you may want to know more details of the course, and the recognition given to the qualification you would obtain, to decide how well it will qualify you to embark on your chosen career. When meeting a company representative on the college 'milk-round' you may be interested in the type of jobs open to graduates, the career structure in the organisation, and how soon after graduation the successful candidates would start work. In applying for membership of a professional association you may ask about the benefits of being a member, or what the association's policy is on topics which concern you.

There is a limit to the number of questions you should ask and the amount of detail you can expect the interviewer to give you. Time will be short and the interviewer is unlikely to have knowledge of every aspect of the job and the organisation. You need to judge for yourself what is appropriate. There are also some questions that you should not ask. 'Have I got the job?' or 'How did I do?', are inappropriate, although you can ask when a decision will be made. Questions on topics totally unrelated to the situation should also be avoided.

Project 4 helps you to list some of the questions you may want to ask.

Presenting yourself effectively

Ideally, every piece of information the interviewer gathers about you during the interview should add to the impression that you are right for the job, or at least should not suggest that you are unsuitable. The interviewer will use this information to decide whether or not you should be selected.

The impression you create is conveyed through:

- your appearance;
- what you say in answer to questions;
- how you structure your answers;
- the way you talk;
- your body movements, posture and facial expressions;
- how you react to what the interviewer says and does;
- your general attitude and manner;
- the questions you ask;
- your performance on any tests and exercises.

To project the best possible image of yourself you need to avoid anything that might create an unfavourable impression and convey only positive qualities. This is not as difficult as it sounds if you prepare carefully.

PREPARING FOR THE INTERVIEW

You have already been asked to prepare lists of the things that you would do in advance of your interview (Activity 2, Projects 1 and 2), and the information given above should have made this clearer.

Activity 7

Before reading on, and using the list above as a guide, write down what you need to know to be able to create a good impression.

Guidelines

You probably thought of the more detailed aspects of your preparation, but there are two fundamental things that you need to know in preparing for your interview:

- what image of yourself you want to project; and
- how to create that image during the interview.

The image you want to project

Project 3 helped you to take the first major step in your preparation by asking you to list the characteristics of the ideal candidate (the personal profile). This tells you approximately what type of person the interviewer is looking for. However, there is no point in trying to project an image totally unlike yourself. If you are successful at the interview you would be expected to sustain that image. The interviewer is also likely to detect that you are putting on an act. Your individuality, provided it does not involve anything which would disqualify you from selection, can also be a major factor in your favour.

The image you project should be an honest reflection of yourself, but one in which you emphasise those characteristics which make you suitable for selection. The personal profile helps you to decide what information about yourself you need to present. If the job calls for a person with good organisational abilities, for example, you need to make sure that the interviewer gets to know about any relevant experience you possess. Later chapters help you to plan what information, and what impression, you want to convey to the interviewer.

Projecting the image

One of the advantages of being yourself at an interview is that it is easier to create a positive impression. You don't have to worry about sustaining a pretence. However, you do need to know how to communicate effectively. Apart from the fact that good communication skills are an asset in most jobs, and sometimes vital, you need them to inform the interviewer of your suitability for the job.

The image you convey in an interview is made up of many different pieces of information from quite different sources. The interviewer builds up a picture of you by putting all this information together to identify specific characteristics. What you tell the interviewer about your experience, for example, could suggest that you enjoy meeting and talking to people. If this is true, then it should also be reflected in your manner and behaviour during the interview.

To present the best possible image of yourself you must be in control of what you are revealing about yourself. The only way to do this effectively is to know what is going to happen during the interview and be prepared to respond in an appropriate way. The following chapters help you to do this.

Key Points

- You must take an active role in your interview to find out if the situation on offer suits you, and to present yourself in the best possible way.

- You can predict what qualities are required in the ideal candidate and decide what impression you want to create.
- Projecting that image involves deciding what information to give about yourself and learning how to communicate it effectively.

 ### Project 4

1. Make a list of all the things that you want out of a job (or the type of situation for which you are applying). Try to make this as broad as possible. For example, it may include helping you to achieve a future ambition, perhaps through the skills or knowledge that you will acquire. You may want to work with a certain type of person, or with a small rather than a large group, or to have good support while you are learning. Or it may be simply a question of money. List anything that you think is important to you.

   The job is very unlikely to provide all of the things that you want, so when you have finished your list, mark those which you feel are *essential* (without which you would not accept an offer).

2. Look at the things you have marked 'essential'. Do you know whether the situation you are applying for provides all of these? If not, outline some questions that you could ask the interviewer to get the information you want. If they are all provided, are there any other topics you would like to know about? Outline some questions that you could ask. Remember that your questions should reflect a keen interest in the job or situation on offer. The list of topics on pages 38–39 gives some ideas.

use of languages
international atmosphere
helping people.
making their stay so good they'll spend entire tslin London

5 ▶ THE INTERVIEW

Uncertainty about what will happen in an interview is usually the major cause of interview nerves. The less candidates know about what will happen the more nervous they are, and the more difficult it is to present themselves well.

The way in which individuals conduct interviews, even within the same organisation, can differ, but the outline presented in this chapter will help you to predict what might happen at your interview.

DIFFERENT TYPES OF INTERVIEW

There are some major differences in the way that the various types of interview are conducted. These are worth noting so that you will know what to expect, and they also make a difference to the type and amount of information you will be required to give.

The one-to-one interview

This is the most common type of interview, consisting of one interviewer talking with each applicant individually. If a single one-to-one interview is used, the interviewer has to gain a complete picture of candidates during this one meeting. This involves covering all the necessary topics in as much detail as time allows. The shorter the interview, the less likely you are to have to talk about any one issue in depth.

When sequential (a series of one-to-one) interviews are used, each one will be slightly different. The first, usually used to eliminate unsuitable candidates, may cover all relevant topics but not in depth. The interviewer will concentrate on finding out whether you have the necessary skills and experience (or potential to acquire them), and less on things such as what makes you tick as a person. Subsequent interviews will be more searching and probably require more detailed answers. You are also likely to be asked questions on a wider variety of topics. If different people are conducting each of the interviews, then their role in the organisation is likely to influence the type of questions they ask.

College or campus interviews are slightly different again. When representatives of an organisation visit a college or university to meet potential recruits, an important part of their job is to 'sell' the idea of working for the organisation. This is becoming increasingly important as the competition for good graduate recruits increases. More than half the interview may be taken up by the interviewer explaining the benefits the organisation can offer. The remainder will be devoted to finding out whether the candidates are the type of people the organisation wants and asking about their plans for the future.

The panel interview

This is more common in the public sector, such as the Civil Service, health authorities and local councils, and consists of a variable number of people (usually from three to six) interviewing together. Panel interviews are not always conducted efficiently. They range from a free-for-all, where the interviewers chip in with any question they can think of as soon as they get the chance, to a very systematic interrogation of the candidates.

If this method is used regularly by the organisation, as in the Civil Service, then the interviewers will take turns to ask questions. Each one will probably concentrate on a particular topic, such as the candidate's experience, or education and training, and ask questions for roughly equal amounts of time. There will often be a chairperson whose role is to run the interview. This may include greeting candidates, asking the first questions, introducing the other interviewers, and asking candidates if they have any questions at the end of the interview.

Panel interviews are also commonly used by large organisations in selecting people for promotion. This may be people who have applied for or been recommended for a specific post, or the interviews may be used to create a list of people suitable for promotion when a suitable vacancy arises. The promotional panel usually has fewer interviewers but they each spend more time asking questions. The interview differs from those where new recruits are involved, because the interviewers already have detailed information on how the individual candidates have performed, and about their experience since joining the organisation. They will want to check the information they have and explore the individual's capacity to cope with a more senior position. This is much more a 'test' of how individuals react and may involve putting the candidates under pressure, for example by asking them to explain or qualify their comments.

THE STAGES OF THE INTERVIEW

The sequence of events that occurs in interviews varies tremendously, depending on the type of interview and the interviewer. Trained interviewers will usually follow some form of plan, although this is not common, while others may approach it haphazardly, without any particular sense of direction. Either way, the interview will include the following stages even though they may not be clearly defined.

Getting there

It is a good idea to treat this as the first stage of your interview. In order to feel calm and unruffled when the interview starts, you need to ensure that there is no last-minute panic in getting to the interview on time. Sometimes the organisation will supply you with a map or directions. If not, you should plan how you are going to get there, consulting maps and timetables if necessary, and ensuring that you allow some extra time for any hold-ups. Take the letter inviting you to the interview with you, so that you are certain of the time and location. It is unwise to get there too early because if you are the anxious type a long wait will give you time to start worrying.

If the interview is being held within easy reach, you could visit the location a few days earlier. This will help you to plan your route and give you an idea of what it will be like on the day.

When you arrive

Normally you will have been told where and to whom you should report. If you get lost, ask for directions from reception or an employee. Try not to waste time searching because it is likely to increase any tension you may be feeling.

Depending on the number of people being interviewed, and whether the interviews are running on time, you may be shown to a waiting area. It is debatable whether, if you have to wait, you should use this time to run through some of the important points you want to get across to the interviewer. For some people this works well, while others simply get more nervous. You will need to judge what is best for you. Reading helps some people to relax. Newspapers, magazines or literature about the organisation may be provided in the waiting area.

When you arrive at the location, and while you are waiting, you may be in the presence of a company employee, such as a receptionist. Although it does not happen frequently, this person may report to the interviewer on individual candidates. So it is wise to think of such people as being involved in the selection process, and make sure that the image you present is one that does not create an unfavourable impression.

The interview setting

Interview locations can vary from a small, quiet room set aside for the purpose to a large open-plan office where employees are continuing, noisily, with their day-to-day work. The majority of interviews are conducted in private. Often the interviewer sits behind a desk, with a seat provided for the candidate on the opposite side or adjacent to the desk. Alternatively the setting may be less formal, with the interviewer and candidate sitting around a low coffee table.

The different settings of interviews can make candidates feel either comfortable and relaxed, or ill at ease. If the interviewer is sitting in a high chair and the candidate in a low one, for example, it emphasizes the interviewer's superior position. A large desk in between the interviewer and the candidate, emphasizing their difference in authority, can also give the interviewer an advantage. These situations are not usually created deliberately, but because the interviewer does not think about the effect it can have on candidates.

At panel interviews, the interviewers may sit in a line behind a desk, or around a table with the candidate. If they are behind a desk, the chair for candidates is often placed several feet away from the other side of the desk. Whatever the setting for the interview, on most occasions interviewers will try to put candidates at their ease. Some tips on how to react under circumstances which you feel are threatening are given in Chapter 6.

Meeting the interviewer

When the time comes for your interview, you may be called into the interview room or the interviewer may come out to greet you. Their first impression of you is very important and is discussed in the next chapter.

Typically, the interviewer's first words will be a greeting and introduction, such as, 'Hello. It's Colin Stokes, isn't it? I'm Rachael Parkes, the personnel officer. Please come in and sit down.' This will obviously vary, and may include thanks for coming, why this person is conducting the interviews, and small talk about subjects such as your journey to the interview.

Activity 8

Before reading the guidelines, list the things you expect to happen from this point until the end of the interview.

Guidelines

It is not possible to predict exactly what will happen in an interview, but all of the following areas may be covered.

Breaking the ice

The majority of interviewers will try to put candidates at their ease at the beginning of the interview, although they will do so with a varying amount of success. They may use small talk (eg about the weather, your journey to the interview, or the day's major news story) or an explanation of the purpose of the interview, how it will be conducted, and how long it will last. You may also be told to feel free to ask questions at any time, or that there will be an opportunity for you to ask questions at the end of the interview.

Even though this initial period may be intended to make you feel more at ease, the interview has started and the interviewer will often be noting your behaviour and responses.

Facts about the job

Interviewers often give information about the job and the organisation early in the interview, the amount of detail depending on how much information you have been given previously. You can often get a better impression of the job and the organisation from what the interviewer says than from something like a job description. Further details may emerge during the course of the interview, when the conversation turns to the type of skills and experience that are required for the job.

Questions, questions, questions

The interviewer's questions may start the moment you both meet, with something like, 'You managed to find us OK, then?' and continue right up to the point that you leave. Remember that every answer you give can tell the interviewer something about yourself. Questions usually take up the major part of the interview – being its most important element – and normally will have begun in earnest within a couple of minutes of the interview starting.

The ways in which interviewers can use questions to build up a picture of candidates, together with the types of question that are usually asked, are described in detail in later chapters.

Your chance to ask questions

Normally, towards the end of the interview, the interviewer will ask if you have any questions. If you are not asked, and there is something you want to know, it is perfectly acceptable to say something like, 'There is something I would like to ask you.' It is highly unlikely that an interviewer would refuse to answer reasonable questions.

Interviewers achieve two things by giving you the opportunity to ask questions. They ensure that you know all you want to know about the job and the organisation, and they can gain clues as to your priorities as far as the job is concerned.

When both of you have finished asking questions the interviewer will end the interview, unless you are required to do any tests or exercises.

Tests and exercises

The use of formal assessment techniques such as personality measures, intelligence tests and group tasks, is not widespread. However, it is becoming more common and you need to know about them. They are used by some large organisations and some public sector bodies. In addition, some organisations require candidates to sit literacy and numeracy tests. If any of these are a regular feature of the organisation's selection procedure you will usually be told, prior to your interview, that you will be assessed in this way. If not, and you would like to check, you can ask someone who knows the organisation whether it uses them.

These techniques take many different forms and can be used during the interview, usually near the end, or outside the interview. Intelligence tests are familiar to many people through books like *Know Your Own IQ*, by H.J. Eysenck. Their content varies depending on what aspect of intelligence is being measured and how they are being used, but each question usually has one right answer. Personality measures commonly consist of questionnaires with multiple-choice answers, none of which is right or wrong. The replies simply give a picture of whichever aspects of the individual's personality are being measured.

Another type of assessment procedure, used most often in selection for senior posts, involves giving candidates a task or range of tasks to perform which relate in some way to the job. This is often used to assess things which are not easily assessed during an interview. One method is to bring several candidates together and give them a situation or problem to discuss on which they must reach a decision or find a solution. Candidates are observed during the discussion and their contributions are noted. Characteristics such as reasoning skills, team working and leadership qualities can be assessed in this way.

Apart from this type of formal assessment technique, you could be given an informal test or exercise to do. If the job involves arithmetic, for example, you could be asked to add up a column of figures. Where interpersonal skills are important, the interviewer may, for example, take on the role of an awkward person that you have to deal with. You could be put in this type of situation at almost any stage of the interview.

Whatever the task you are given, *the following points may help you.*

Firstly, it is very unlikely that selection will be based solely on the results of this assessment; they are usually used to supplement the information gained from the interviews. It is also vitally important to listen to, or read carefully, the instructions you are given. Apart from the likelihood that you will make mistakes if you don't, it reflects badly on you if you appear not to understand what are usually simple instructions. Where there is a time limit, estimate first how much time you have available to spend on each part of the task. That way you won't find yourself completing only a small part of it, or rushing through without much care just to finish it. Try to concentrate on what you are doing, ignoring any observers or whatever else may distract you. If you are answering a multiple-choice questionnaire, avoid the temptation to choose answers simply because you think they will create a good impression. These techniques have become very sophisticated and when your answers are analysed it is likely that your strategy will be quite obvious. Finally, if you have the opportunity, work through some of the intelligence and personality tests that you can find in books on the subject.

Sometimes, after doing this type of test, you will be given an idea of how well you did. However you feel, delighted or disappointed about your performance or the feedback you have been given, try not to show your feelings. Being over-confident can create as poor an impression as pessimism.

The end of the interview

The length of your interview will vary depending on the interviewer and the situation. It ranges from around 20 minutes for a first job, or the first in a series of interviews, to an hour or more for a senior position, or a final selection interview.

If your expenses for attending the interview are being paid by the organisation, the interviewer may explain how to claim these or check that you have received them.

The interviewer may comment on your performance in the interview or how well you are suited to the job. You may be told, there and then, whether you have been successful or not. If you are unsuccessful you should be told the reasons. If not, ask politely why you have been rejected. The answer you get may help you in your next interview. Alternatively, you may be told when you can expect a decision. If the interviewer doesn't say, it is reasonable for you to ask. You could be told that further interviews will take place with shortlisted candidates, and when these will be held.

Finally, the interviewer will thank you for coming and may see you you out. Remember that it is only when you leave the interviewer that the interview has ended. Up until then you are still being assessed.

Interviews and interviewers vary so much that it is impossible to predict how closely your interview will follow this pattern. It may follow a set plan or be completely haphazard. The interviewer may appear friendly and chatty, or stern and rather formal. If you go to your interview with a fixed image of what it will be like then you can almost guarantee that something will happen to surprise you. If you approach it with an open mind, prepared for whatever could happen, you will feel more confident and be better able to exploit any situation.

Key Points

- If you know what to expect in your interview you will be able to prepare more thoroughly and therefore feel more relaxed and confident on the day.
- There are a number of things which happen in almost every interview, although the order in which they happen can vary.
- If you go to your interview prepared for whatever could happen, not expecting it to follow a particular format, you will be able to take full advantage of the opportunities to present yourself well.

Project 5

In this project you are asked to find out more about the job (or situation) and the organisation. You should be able to find a large amount of information and the following questions will give you an idea of the type of thing to look for.

- What is the business of the organisation?
- What divisions does it have and where are they located?
- What is the purpose of the department to which you are applying?
- What type of people does the organisation employ – generally and in the department to which you are applying?
- Does the job involve contact with people from outside the organisation, or people at a higher level within it?
- What type of interview does the organisation usually use when recruiting for this type of post?
- What is the position within the organisation of the person who will interview you?
- What type of public and professional image does the organisation have?
- Has the organisation been in the news recently?

For situations other than a job you will be seeking different information. For example, does the college or university specialise in any particular subjects? What are people who graduated in the past few years doing now? Are there any links with commercial and industrial organisations? What is the association's position on (a subject which concerns you)?

Many more questions will probably spring to mind as you carry out your research. It will help you if you bear in mind how you will use this information, which is to:

- show, during the interview, that you are interested in the situation on offer and that you know what it involves;
- get a better idea of the qualities required in the ideal candidate;
- decide what type of interview you are likely to be given;
- decide whether there are any questions you want to ask the interviewer.

These are some of the sources of information that you might find useful:

- publications on careers and careers training;
- careers advisers and careers officers;
- school teachers;
- information published by the organisation eg house journals, annual reports, educational material;
- course prospectuses;
- people within the organisation;
- friends, relatives and colleagues;
- diverse publications in reference libraries.

If, as a result of your research, any further questions come to mind that you would like to ask the interviewer, add them to your list from Project 4.

6 ▶ HOW YOU WILL BE ASSESSED

Some interviewers are very skilled at finding out what candidates are like, others find it very difficult; the majority are somewhere in between. Skilled interviewers can tap many more sources of information about you than those who are unskilled and who rely on more limited information. To be well prepared you need to know the ways in which you could be assessed. This chapter examines how you communicate information to the interviewer and what you need to do to present yourself in the best way.

 Activity 9

Before reading the guidelines, briefly describe the impression an interviewer might gain of a candidate who does the following.

1. Breezes into the interview room looking untidy.
2. Hesitates for a long time and then answers a slightly different question to the one asked.
3. Speaks so quietly that it is almost impossible to hear what is being said.
4. Speaks loudly, gestures broadly with the arms and repeatedly comments on irrelevant topics.
5. Sprawls in the chair with arms hanging limply at the side.
6. Shows a surprised expression when asked to talk about an interest expressed earlier in the interview.

7. Becomes very nervous when asked to explain the reasons for leaving a previous job.

Guidelines

These situations relate to some of the ways in which an interviewer can gain an impression of, and assess, candidates. This impression can vary depending on what has happened earlier in the interview and how these situations arise. However, you may have written something along these lines.

1. The fact that the candidate appears confident while looking untidy suggests that it is not unusual for this person to look that way.
2. Hesitating a long time and then not answering the question that was asked suggests that either the candidate does not want to answer the question – perhaps because there is something to hide – or was not listening.
3. Speaking unreasonably quietly suggests that the candidate either lacks confidence or does not want the interviewer to hear the answer.
4. This show of confidence could be an attempt to overcome nervousness, or the candidate may normally be brash and outspoken.
5. This over-relaxed, somewhat lifeless way of sitting, could indicate over-confidence or lack of interest in the interview and the job.
6. Showing surprise when asked to talk about a subject which has been claimed to be an interest suggests that the claim was not true, and may have been said simply for effect.
7. An increase in nervousness suggests that the reasons for the candidate leaving the previous job are not favourable, whatever explanation is given.

These examples are not necessarily an accurate reflection of the candidate but the interviewer can wrongly assume what the behaviour means. The important point is that the candidate can create a poor impression.

HOW YOU CREATE AN IMPRESSION

Although candidates' answers to questions provide the interviewer with most of the information required to make a selection, this is not the only source on which a judgement of their suitability can be made. If information from other sources is strongly unfavourable it can outweigh the positive information given in answer to questions.

Not all interviewers will consciously note information from all of the sources described below. However, it can register unconsciously and create a strong general impression. This impression may be the deciding factor when the interviewer makes a selection.

First impressions

It is well established that first impressions, although they are frequently inaccurate, tend to be long-lasting and difficult to change. The first few minutes of the interview could well determine the impression that you leave with the interviewer. If you are late for the interview, for example, even of you have the best of excuses, the first impression you create (before you explain) will be poor. Your manner and appearance when you first meet the interviewer will have a similar impact, no matter what happens later.

Your answers to questions

What you say in answer to questions helps to confirm (or refute) the information already available about you, gives more facts about your experience, interests and ambitions, and gives an indication of things like your depth of knowledge, maturity, and ability to communicate. The type of information you give, the amount, and the way that you phrase it, helps the interviewer to build up a picture of you. This subject is examined in detail in Chapters 7 and 8, but it is important to remember that it is not only *what* you say that gives information, but also *how* you say it.

How you speak

Recall recent telephone conversations you have had and it is obvious how much information you can gather from the way people speak. You can often tell, for example, whether they are nervous or confident, enthusiastic or bored, shy or bold. Shyness and nervousness can be reflected in speaking quietly, mumbling, or hesitation; showing no emotion in the voice can signify boredom or tiredness.

Another source of information is the *combination* of what you are saying and how you say it. For example, if you are giving details of experience that you don't have, in order to create a good impression, and constantly hesitate, your deception may be quite obvious to the interviewer. Similarly, if you speak in a dull monotone when talking about an aspect of the job you say you will enjoy, the two sources of information – what you say and how you say it – conflict and don't ring true.

Strong accents, whether regional or national, at one time could have had a strong influence on interviewers. Today they have much less impact provided the person can be understood easily.

Your attitude and manner

Irrespective of what you say, the type of person you are shows in such things as the way you speak, move and respond to the interviewer, your posture and facial expressions. Are you brash and outspoken, or quiet and thoughtful? Are you bright and enthusiastic, or sullen and uninterested? Are you trying hard to impress, or are you being yourself. Are you easily provoked and argumentative, or quiet and controlled? Do you have a sense of humour, or are you serious and intense? Are you strong and assertive, or meek and passive? Your general attitude and manner constitutes an important part of the impression you create.

Body language

If you turn down the sound on the television and watch people talking, it is surprising how much information about them comes across in the way that they look and move. When we are talking we are usually unaware of our non-verbal behaviour, or body language – our posture, movement, gestures, facial expressions and eye-contact with other people. We are also unaware, usually, of other people's body language, although it does create an unconscious impression on us. We are used to speaking only the thoughts that we want others to hear. This is not true of our body language and we can stay things unconsciously with our body which we would rather not reveal.

There is conflicting evidence about the importance of body language in determining the impression you create in an interview. However, some interviewers are skilled at observing candidates in this way, and you should be aware of what you may be 'saying' with your body. For example, sitting rigidly upright, with your hands tightly gripping the arm rests of your chair, gives the impression of nervousness; constantly shifting about in your chair can also reflect nervousness, as well as irritation or boredom: fidgeting, drumming your fingers, or turning away, can all suggest lack of interest and attention; sitting sprawled in the chair with your legs crossed can signal over-confidence or lack of interest. All of these impressions can be created irrespective of what you are saying.

Certain mannerisms, when repeated often, can also be distracting and irritating. Obviously it depends on the interviewer, but things such as repeatedly straightening your tie, pulling down the hem of your skirt, biting your nails, scratching your head, tugging on the lobe of your ear, tapping your feet and making sweeping gestures with your arms, can have a negative effect. You need to avoid anything which conflicts with, or distracts the interviewer from, what you are saying, or which creates a poor impression.

Facial expression

Our face mirrors everything that we feel, from the slightest feeling of unease to full-blown rage. Most of this is involuntary, the muscles in our face reacting automatically to our thoughts and emotions. It sends out a constant stream of messages – with a smile, a frown, a quizzical look – which betray what we are thinking and feeling. A fixed, lifeless expression may reflect unease or boredom. A blank expression, a frown, or a grimace when asked a question, all reveal our feelings about that question. The changing look on our face reflects whether we are attentive or uninterested, and whether we understand or not. It is important to know what the expression on your face is telling the interviewer.

Eye-contact

When two people are talking they periodically look each other straight in the eye. This is called eye-contact and is usually automatic. We look to see if the other person is listening, and to note the response. The other person looks at us to show attention and to note any non-verbal signals we are sending. When we stop talking we look at the other person in anticipation of a response. This process is repeated in a consistent way during most conversations.

The pattern of eye-contact people show during a conversation reveals how they feel about each other, about the situation, and about the subject of the conversation. Suddenly looking away when the interviewer asks a particular question could mean that this is a delicate subject for the candidate. A fixed stare is unnatural, unnerving and distracting. Avoiding eye-contact altogether can reflect lack of interest, embarrassment or nervousness. So the pattern of your eye-contact with the interviewer affects the impression you are creating.

Nervousness

Most interviewers accept that some nervousness is almost inevitable in an interview, and the majority will try to make candidates feel at their ease. Being slightly nervous can be beneficial because it keeps you alert and better able to respond to the interviewer. If you are too relaxed, perhaps through over-confidence, your mind will not be as sharp and you are likely to be a little careless in what you say and do.

On the other hand, being too nervous creates a number of problems. Tension above a certain level will make you feel uncomfortable and less confident. It will be more difficult to concentrate and you may not listen to questions carefully; you may be so anxious to reply to questions that you don't think carefully before you answer; and you may have trouble speaking clearly.

A sudden visible increase in your nervousness can also indicate that the interviewer has touched upon a subject which is delicate and which you would rather not talk about. So it is important, for a variety of reasons, to be able to control your nervousness.

Your personal appearance

The way you are dressed and your personal appearance has an immediate impact on the interviewer. Although it is not such a critical factor as it may have been in the past, it can still be a major influence. Faced with the choice of two candidates who are very similar in other ways – one tidily dressed and well groomed, the other untidy and too casually dressed – the interviewer will almost certainly choose the former.

The impression your appearance creates also colours the interviewer's perception of what happens during the interview. For example, someone who is untidy and gives muddled answers to questions may appear generally 'sloppy'. However, if someone who is well groomed and neatly dressed gives muddled answers it is more likely to be put down to nervousness.

Personal appearance and style of dress may also be important in the job. Someone who will be meeting the company's clients or the public, for example, is representing the company and would need to be 'presentable'. If candidates have not taken care over their appearance for the interview, it is reasonable for the interviewer to assume that their attitude would be the same in the job. It could also suggest to the interviewer that they are not seriously interested in the job.

Because of the impact it can have, you must give serious consideration to your personal appearance.

The questions you ask

The questions you ask the interviewer say a lot about you. They can reveal whether you are interested in the job and the organisation, what aspects appeal to you, whether you have been attentive during the interview, and how well you have understood what you have been told. For example, if you ask what the basic duties of the job are, when this will almost certainly have been explained already (by the interviewer and perhaps in the advertisement and literature from the organisation), it will appear that you are either uninterested or you have not been listening. Similarly, if your questions concentrate on the sports facilities provided by the organisation, the interviewer could feel that the job is of secondary importance to you. Not asking any questions can also suggest that you don't care, and so you should be prepared to ask at least a couple of questions.

Questions on irrelevant topics, when time is short, can irritate the interviewer. Asking for more detailed information than is necessary can have a similar effect. So too can questions which challenge something the interviewer has said, unless they are phrased carefully. You should not ask questions about how well you have done.

Tests and other assessment techniques

It is worth emphasising here that a selection decision is rarely based solely on the results of assessment tests and exercises. The impact you create when talking to the interviewer is usually much more important.

HOW THE INTERVIEWER CONSTRUCTS A PICTURE OF YOU

If a candidate answers a slightly different question to the one asked, or shifts nervously in the chair while answering, it suggests that the candidate may be uneasy about the subject of the question. Good interviewers will, if the subject is important, probe until they are satisfied that they have a clear picture of the situation. Similarly, if two different pieces of information conflict – perhaps the candidate claims to be able to handle new situations well but shows a lack of confidence, or claims to be easy to get on with but has changed jobs frequently – then the interviewer will try to find out which piece of information is true.

By comparing all the information from different sources, and probing deeper when things are unclear, interviewers can build up a fairly accurate picture of each candidate. It is therefore important to think about the complete image that you will create and not just individual aspects of your performance.

WHAT IMPRESSION WILL YOU CREATE?

Provided that you do not try deliberately to mislead the interviewer by pretending to have qualities you do not have simply to get the job, it is relatively straightforward to present yourself in a positive way.

 ### Activity 10

Before reading the guidelines, briefly describe how you can create a positive impression in your interview through:

(1) the way that you enter the interview room; (2) how you speak; (3) your attitude and manner; (4) how you sit in your chair; and (5) your general appearance.

 ### Guidelines

Although some of the things which reflect a 'positive' image will be specific to the situation for which you are being interviewed, there are many which are the same whatever the situation.

Meeting the interviewer

You should make an extra effort when you meet the interviewer to ensure that the first impression you create is a good one. Depending on the situation and setting, you should:

- close the door behind you when you have entered the interview room;
- walk steadily to the chair provided for you, glancing at the interviewer with a smile of acknowledgement;
- wait to be asked to sit down;

- be prepared to shake hands if the interviewer initiates it;
- look the interviewer in the eye and smile. At a board interview, do the same with each interviewer in turn as you are introduced (try to remember their names because you may want to use them later).

Overall, you should appear relaxed, pleasant and pleased to be there.

Speaking

You will be doing most of the talking in your interview, mostly in answer to the interviewer's questions. To use your voice effectively you should

- speak up, in a clear and confident-sounding voice;
- pace the speed at which you speak – people tend to speak too quickly when they are nervous;
- let your voice show enthusiasm;
- if you have a very strong accent, make an extra effort to speak clearly and, if necessary, more slowly.

Chapter 9 includes advice on practising how you will speak in your interview.

Your attitude and manner

This is an area where the characteristics of the ideal candidate may partly determine what type of image you want to create. It will generally not be *different* characteristics which you need to show, but the *degree* to which you show them.

These are the sort of questions you need to answer:

How strongly should I assert myself?
In most situations you should let the interviewer control the interview. This is not to say that you should be passive; you must show that you are involved. You should appear modest in terms of 'selling' yourself, unless you are asked something like, 'What makes you think you are suitable for this job?'

However, if the job calls for someone who is strong and assertive, perhaps a sales position, then you should look for opportunities to exhibit these characteristics. For example, if you have finished answering a question and have a related point you would like to raise, you could take this opportunity to lead the conversation. You can also show these qualities very effectively by being confident and bold in expressing your ideas, and by defending them if they are challenged by the interviewer (provided that they are sound). You should always be agreeable when doing this, and not appear domineering or argumentative.

How much confidence should I show?
Self-confidence is an essential quality to show in all interviews, although too much confidence is unappealing and will not be in your favour. It is difficult to reflect confidence – in a firm and steady voice, relaxed manner and posture – when you are feeling nervous. Preparation and rehearsal are the best ways to ensure that you feel confident in your interview, and if you *feel* confident you will automatically *show* confidence.

How enthusiastic should I be?
It is as bad to be bubbling over with excitement in an interview as it is to sit looking bored. However, you must appear keen and show enthusiasm for the job. This is reflected in the things you say, your tone of voice and your body language. Recalling what you are like when talking about something that really interests you will give you an idea of how you can show your enthusiasm.

Should I be serious or lighthearted?
You must take the interview seriously and not be flippant, but you should not sit with a serious expression on your face throughout the interview. The best attitude to adopt is one of interest and enjoyment. Showing that you have a sense of humour, if the occasion arises, is a good idea, but laughter (even a nervous laugh) at the wrong moment, or in excess, can give a poor impression. Do not try to introduce humour yourself, unless it is something that you often do, and do well, and then only if the interviewer is the type to appreciate it and the moment is right.

Overall, your manner should be pleasant and agreeable.

Your body language

Your posture should reflect interest and a relaxed and confident manner. Get yourself comfortable as soon as you sit down, so that you don't need to shift about later. Choose a position which is comfortable (it will help you to relax) but not one which makes you look slovenly. Whatever type of chair you are given, try to sit upright and lean forward slightly (this shows you are interested and attentive). Don't sit rigid throughout the interview, but avoid shifting about too much (like swaying or wriggling in your seat).

When we are nervous we tend to do things with our hands and arms which can both irritate and distract the interviewer and give information about how we feel. As soon as you sit down, find a comfortable position for your arms and hands. Avoid moving them about too much, either shifting position or making too many or too large gestures. Avoid all of the things which people do when they are nervous – fiddling with a pen, tapping fingers, biting nails, head scratching, and so on.

Your facial expression

Facial expressions arise naturally from the way we are feeling. For example, when we are listening to someone we periodically smile automatically in recognition of what is being said. If you feel relaxed and interested and are attentive, then it will show in your face.

Eye-contact

Eye-contact with the interviewer is important; you should not stare or avoid the interviewer's gaze. Look the interviewer in the eye as you first meet (in recognition), most of the time when the interviewer is talking (to show that you are listening), and periodically when you are talking (which reinforces the communication). Do not stare into space or fix your gaze somewhere in the room. Like your facial expression, eye-contact happens automatically. If you feel relaxed and confident you should have no problems.

Controlling nervousness

There are a wide variety of ways of dealing with nervousness. Preparation and rehearsal, which helps to build your confidence, is probably the best way, but there are also many relaxation techniques. If you feel you would benefit by learning how to use these, books are available on the subject.

The following methods may help you during the interview:

- make sure you are sitting comfortably;
- don't feel that you have to answer questions immediately – take a few seconds at least to think;

- listen carefully to the interviewer – it can cause you to panic if you are asked to reply to something you have not understood;
- if the interviewer asks you to explain something you have said, don't feel that you have said something wrong;
- if the interviewer seems to be putting pressure on you, don't feel that it is personal – it is just to test how you cope under stress;
- try to think of the interview as an opportunity to show how capable you are, rather than as a 'testing', threatening situation.

Bear in mind the following points: you are in with a chance; the interviewer is doing a job and you can help do that job; the interview is a challenge just like any other new thing you do; the interviewer is not judging you as a friend but as someone who may be able to help the organisation.

Drinking alcohol, smoking and chewing gum are used to help people relax. None of these is appropriate for your interview. On no account have a drink before an interview. Apart from dulling your thinking, the smell of alcohol will not impress the interviewer. Don't smoke or chew gum during the interview. Even if the interviewer invites you to smoke, try to do without one if this is not going to affect your performance.

Your personal appearance

The most important thing, in terms of your appearance, is to show that you have taken some care over it. The situation for which you are applying and the type of organisation will give you clues about how smartly you should dress, but over-dressing should be avoided as much as under-dressing. There is some debate about whether you should purposely dress in the same way as employees of the organisation. Some interviewers appreciate it, while others think that it is inappropriate, particularly for young people early in their careers. The safest option is simply to make sure that you are clean, smart and tidy. This includes your clothes, hair, fingernails and shoes.

Another important consideration is to avoid anything which could make you feel uncomfortable – clothes which are too thick or thin, or too tight, or new clothes which make you feel self-conscious.

Some of the factors discussed above may seem relatively unimportant. However, taken together they can add considerably to your chances of success or failure. A little time spent thinking about them is very worthwhile.

Key Points

- In addition to your answers to questions, interviewers can use a variety of other sources of information during the interview to assess you.
- You need to understand the ways in which you communicate information about yourself – both positive and negative.
- Presenting yourself effectively involves controlling the image you create through your words, actions and appearance.

 Project 6

This project is based on the research you did for Project 5 and the personal profile you compiled in Project 3. Look at your notes from Project 5.

1. What does your research tell you about the knowledge, skills and personal characteristics that could be required in this situation? For example, do most of the employees dress formally? Will it be important for you to dress well because of contact with people outside the organisation, or with senior executives inside the organisation? What sort of image is appropriate for this situation/profession? Does the organisation have any policies which you would have to observe (eg no smoking in the office)? What type of people are normally accepted in this type of situation? What skills and knowledge do they have normally? What opinions and ambitions is it appropriate to have?
2. What is the next career step for someone in this situation, what qualities would be required and how would this advancement be achieved? For example, what additional skills and knowledge are needed for advancement? Is it the type of organisation which would want people who are ambitious, or people who are less anxious to advance? Does advancement require special training, or acquiring formal qualifications?
3. Is the interviewer likely to have any particular bias due to his or her position within the organisation? (See page 24.)

Your answers to these types of question will tell you more about the type of person required for the situation. Make a list of all the relevant characteristics. When you have done that, look at the personal profile you compiled in Project 3 and add any characteristics which are missing.

Finally, what type of interview are you likely to be given: one-to-one, panel, sequential (short-listing, intermediary or final assessment)?

7 ▶ WHAT QUESTIONS WILL YOU BE ASKED?

Generally, the most worrying aspect of being interviewed is being unsure of how well you will be able to answer questions when put on the spot. It is not possible to know with any certainty what questions you will be asked, but you can do a lot to prepare. For example, you can learn to recognise why an interviewer is asking a particular question and what type of answer is required; you can familiarise yourself with the type of questions generally asked, and predict the topics that are likely to be covered in your interview.

HOW INTERVIEWERS USE QUESTIONS

For reasons explained earlier, interviewers cannot ask candidates outright if they have the qualities required. Instead, they have to encourage them to reveal this information through their answers to a variety of more general questions. At the same time they have to ensure that they get a complete and accurate picture of each individual.

Activity 11

Think about all the ways in which you have heard questions used, and have used them yourself, to obtain information. Write down an example of each type and explain how each is used before reading on.

Guidelines

Irrespective of the topic of conversation, interviewers can use questions

66

in a variety of ways to probe and prompt candidates until they get the information they require. The main methods of doing this can be grouped under the following headings.

Checking

Interviewers can check the accuracy of the information they are given by candidates – both in application forms and during the interview – by asking indirect questions. If candidates are asked about their experience, for example, with a question like, 'Could you explain to me what is involved in compiling those budgets?', their answer and general response can give an indication of whether or not they have the experience they claim. Interviewers can also use questions to check that they have understood what a candidate has said, by asking for clarification.

Clarifying

It is important that interviewers understand what candidates mean by what they say. If they are uncertain they can ask for clarification, either directly – for example by saying, 'Could you explain to me again how you think that situation arose?' – or by paraphrasing what the candidate has said:

Candidate I'd rather be in the office than out on the road.

Interviewer Are you saying that you don't want to have to do much travelling?

Candidate No, it's just that I enjoy working with other people.

Paraphrasing, or reflecting

By restating, in their own words, what candidates have said, interviewers can check and clarify information, and help candidates to see gaps in their explanations and encourage them to explain further. For example:

Interviewer Why do you dislike that part of your job?

Candidate Well, it's something I've got to do every week and I find it quite difficult because I haven't really had the chance to learn it properly.

Interviewer If you do the job every week why haven't you had the opportunity to learn how to do it?

Candidate It's not so much the time ... I just haven't been given any guidance.

Focusing

When you meet people for the first time it is difficult to know what aspects of their experience will reveal their true self. For example, how could you know that someone's performance on a particular task in the past would reveal that person's tendency to get flustered under pressure?

When you have only a short time to talk, as interviewers do, you need to get at the relevant information fairly quickly. Focusing is a powerful probing technique for doing this. The interviewer starts with a general question and then asks a succession of increasingly specific questions, according to the candidate's reply. For example:

Interviewer   What do you enjoy most in your current job?

Candidate   I think it's probably the people I work with.

Interviewer   What is it that you like about them?

Candidate   They are very helpful and easy to get on with.

Interviewer   Do you need to call on them for help very often?

This type of questioning enables interviewers to uncover information which they may otherwise not know exists.

Summarising

Interviewers build up a picture of candidates piece by piece, trying to recognise common threads in the many things they have said. If a particular characteristic is supported by several comments a candidate makes, the interviewer can assume that the person has this characteristic. However, if there is not sufficient information to do this, the interviewer can summarise what candidates have said to help them see gaps in their explanation. For example:

Interviewer   You said that your supervisor encourages people to use their initiative, but aren't you suggesting now that on this occasion you were criticised for showing initiative?

Candidate   Well, perhaps that was because I'd left the telephone unattended for half an hour to sort out the problem.

Interviewers can also summarise to check an assumption. For example:

Interviewer   You started the department's theatre club but handed over the running to someone else soon afterwards; and you took an active part in reorganising the record systems, although you say you don't like maintaining the records. It seems to me that you are happier when things are changing and don't particularly like routine work. Is that a fair comment?

Exerting pressure

Some interviewers use questions to put candidates under pressure to see how they cope. There is disagreement about whether coping with this type of pressure bears any relation to coping with work pressures, but some interviewers use the technique. For example:

Interviewer	So you don't think that you should have to follow your manager's advice?
Candidate	Well, on this occasion I was doing the job and I knew that it would be better to do it my own way.
Interviewer	So are you saying that you know better than someone who has far more experience than you?
Candidate	This time I think I did.
Interviewer	So you don't think experience counts for anything?

Silence

Periods of silence in a conversation, particularly in a situation like an interview, can make us feel very uncomfortable. We feel as if we ought to be saying something to fill the gap. Simply by remaining silent when candidates stop talking, interviewers can encourage them to continue and explain further.

Playing down

If candidates say or intimate something which obviously reflects unfavourably on them, interviewers have the choice of either asking about it openly or playing it down. If they ask a direct question the candidate is likely to be defensive and not say much. If, on the other hand, the interviewer seems to place little importance on it, by the choice of the next question, the candidate is more likely to continue talking about the situation. For example, if someone has been disciplined in a job for serious misconduct, and the interviewer wants to know the reasons, instead of asking, 'Why were you disciplined?', the interviewer could ask something like, 'Are the company's rules and regulations particularly strict then?' The latter question, although not asking 'why' directly, is much more likely to get the candidate to talk honestly about the situation and to reveal the reasons.

As well as being able to use questions in these different ways, interviewers can also use different *types* of question.

DIFFERENT TYPES OF QUESTION

Consider these two questions. Do you think you can do this job well? Why do you think you can do this job well? Both these are on the same subject and sound similar, but they encourage a totally different response. The first (called a *closed* question) can be answered with a simple 'yes' or 'no'. The second (called an *open-ended* question) forces the candidate to give a broader, more informative answer.

Good interviewers ask open-ended questions most of the time. They usually begin with the words, who, what, why, when, where or how, and encourage the candidate to do most of the talking, helping the interviewer to get a lot of information in a short time. Although candidates may not always answer a closed question with just a 'yes' or 'no', they almost always give a short, uninformative reply. However, closed questions can be useful in certain situations, for example to check facts which don't need elaboration, or to curb a particularly talkative candidate when time is short.

A particular type of open-ended question propular with interviewers is the *self-assessment question*, which asks candidates to assess their own strengths and weaknesses in a particular area. For example: Why do you think you can do this job well? What positive qualities do you think you will bring to this job? What do you think you will find most difficult to do in this job? What qualities of yours do you think made your supervisor recommend you for promotion? What makes you think you will be able to handle meetings confidently?

A less common type of question is where the interviewer asks how you would react in a *hypothetical situation*. For example: what would you do if you forgot an important appointment with a customer and, as a result, he decided to cancel a large order? These are of doubtful value in determining how a person would deal with the real situation, but they are asked occasionally.

Leading questions are also of little value in getting accurate information about candidates. These are the type where the interviewer indicates the type of answer expected, or the 'favourable' answer. For example: the job involves a lot of contact with the public; would you enjoy that?

A type of question which can cause confusion for candidates is the *multiple question*. Most interviewers at some time inadvertently ask a string of questions in one sentence, so that the candidate is either unsure of what is being asked or does not know which part to answer first. For example: What parts of the job do you think you are best suited for; do you think you will find it relatively easy to settle down, or are there any aspects of it which may cause you a problem? Although interviewers may recognise that they have asked a multiple question, they do not often clarify which question they want answered.

 Activity 12

What type of information do you think an interviewer could gain from candidates' answers to the following questions?

1. Why did you choose to do these subjects at school?
2. What things do you think you have done particularly well in your current job? What makes you think that?
3. What appeals to you about this job?

 Guidelines

The information candidates give in answer to these questions will obviously vary from person to person, but the interviewer can gain a surprising amount of general information about each individual. For example:

1. The reasons for candidates' choice of subjects at school can reveal their general interests, their career intentions (if any), what motivates them, and their intellectual aptitudes.
2. Candidates' interpretations of what they feel they have done well, and their reasons, can reveal a large range of information, including the standards of performance they feel happy with, their motivation, what they find rewarding, their aptitudes for certain types of work, and their personal ideals.
3. What candidates say appeals to them in the job can reveal things such as the type of work situations they enjoy, what interests and motivates them, and how much they know about the job and organisation.

If you think about how you might answer just these three questions you will see more clearly how they can give the interviewer a large amount of information. Although you may not be giving 'hard' facts, you are revealing a lot about the type of person you are.

THE QUESTIONS YOU COULD BE ASKED

There is an enormous range of questions that an interviewer could ask you and it would be unrealistic to prepare for each of these individually. However, all of the questions will fall into one of these groups of topics:

- education and training;
- work history and experience;
- interests;
- ambitions and motivation;
- job and organisation;
- general topics;
- specialist and technical topics;
- family background and circumstances;
- health.

You can narrow down the topics that you will be questioned on even further. For example, you won't be asked about technical subjects if you are going for a non-technical job; you are unlikely to be asked much about school if you have several years' job experience behind you; you can't be asked about your previous job if this if your first job application; it is unlikely that you will be asked detailed questions about your interests unless it is going to reveal some relevant information, and so on. This makes the task of preparation a little less daunting.

You can narrow down the field again by considering what it is the interviewer is trying to find out, that is, whether or not you have the qualities required. If the company is looking for a good organiser, for example, you can be pretty sure that some of the questions will be directed at finding out if you have shown any aptitude for organisation. Project 7 will help you to use this method to predict the type of questions you could be asked.

You can also sometimes get clues from the application form. If it asks for details of your family, for instance, or your hobbies, or whether you are a member of any professional body, there is usually a reason and the interviewer could well ask you for further information. What other people have told you about the questions they were asked at interviews with the organisation will also give you clues. And your research about the job and the organisation can tell you if there are any topics in which they may be particularly interested.

It is impractical to cover here all of the possible questions. However, the examples listed below will give you an idea of the type of questions that arise most frequently under each subject heading. These are likely to contain many of those you will be asked, although they may not be phrased in exactly the same way. With some thought you will be able to adapt them to your own situation and probably think of many more besides.

Your aim in preparing for your interview is to feel confident in being able to answer any question. This means becoming familiar with the type of questions that are asked, and getting used to putting your thoughts together and expressing them clearly in an answer. Chapter 9 outlines how you can practise doing this, using a list of questions that you will prepare in Project 7.

Education and training

This category includes school, college and university studies, and other formal training courses. The emphasis placed on this topic will depend on how much work experience you have. If you have little or none, then this is the interviewer's major source of information. A lot of the information may be available already from sources like your application form and curriculum vitae, but some questions may be asked to confirm these details, about examination grades, course contents, and so on. These will be fairly straightforward.

However, there are many other questions you may be asked, particularly if you have little work experience to talk about. These can reveal a lot about you as a person. For example:

- Why did you choose to do maths at advanced level when you had done much better in languages at the lower grade?
- Did you consider doing anything other than going to college? Why did you choose not to do that?
- What do you think were the best/weakest parts of the course? Why?
- How do you think it could have been improved?
- At that time, what were you thinking you would like to do when you left?
- What subjects were you best/weakest at? What do you think were the reasons for this?
- What subjects did you like most/least? Why?
- Do you think your results are a good reflection of your abilities? Why?
- What languages do you speak? How well?
- Did you do any projects? Can you tell me about it?
- Do you intend to continue your education?
- What lessons do you think it taught you which will be useful in your life?

- What careers advice have you sought?
- Were there any activities you particularly enjoyed outside of studying? Will you tell me about that? What about it appealed to you?
- What did you do in the school holidays? Could you tell me about that?

Work history and experience

This category covers periods of unemployment and job-hopping, as well as part-time and full-time jobs. With candidates who have many years' work experience, questions in this area are likely to dominate the interview. They will usually concentrate on the most recent and/or most relevant jobs. School and college leavers, with no full-time work experience, may have experience of vacation work and this may be explored, although not as thoroughly as a full-time job. Reasons for unemployment, and how candidates used their time during that period, and reasons for having had several jobs, none of them lasting very long, may also be explored.

Interviewers will have a varying amount of information in this area already, depending on the detail that was requested on the application form, given in your curriculum vitae, and so on. However, they need to identify the relevance of candidates' previous work experience to the situation on offer, and so need to explore that experience quite extensively. As well as the work that has been done, they will be interested in the wider aspects of their experience, such as how well they got on with colleagues, what they thought of the management, how they felt about different aspects of the work, and so on. They will also try to identify trends in candidates' work experience, such as their reasons for the job choices they have made, and how they have developed through their experience.

The following examples show the wide variety of questions that interviewers may ask in this area, but the list is by no means comprehensive. Many of these questions can relate to part-time as well as full-time jobs.

- Why did you choose to work for/leave that company?
- Which of your jobs have you found most interesting? Why? What did it involve?
- What skills and other qualities were needed in that job?
- What aspects of the job did you like best/least? Why?

- What were your main difficulties in the job? How did you deal with them?
- How did you get on with your colleagues?
- What did you do in that job that you see being relevant to this job?
- Were you given any extra responsibility or promoted while you were in the job? Why do you think that was?
- What experience do you have of leading/managing/supervising others?
- Do you ever take work home?
- How much do you know about desktop publishing/any other relevant topic?
- Do you think your progress in the job accurately reflects your abilities?
- How do you think your manager rated your performance on the job? What signs of that did you have?
- What kind of people do you like/dislike to work with? Why?
- What things would you like to avoid in a job? Why?
- Can you describe your ideal boss?
- What is your current/last salary?
- What salary are you seeking?
- Can we approach your employer for a reference?
- Are you considering any other offers at the moment? What are they?
- How much notice do you have to give?
- Why have you stayed in one job for so long? Why do you want to change now?
- Why have you changed jobs so often?
- Do you think having changed jobs so often is a hindrance in getting another job?
- How did you feel about being unemployed?
- What did you do with your time while you were unemployed?
- Why were you dismissed?
- If you do not get this job, what will do you do then?

Interests

This category covers a number of areas – intellectual, physical, practical, artistic and social. Not all interviewers will ask questions in this category, although it is particularly popular when candidates have little work experience and when the selection procedure is rigorous. If interviewers have information on candidates' interests, the questions can cover any aspect of those; if not, they would start with a general question.

In asking these questions the interviewer may be trying to find out a variety of things, such as whether your claims about your interests are true; how deep an interest you have; whether you prefer physical or intellectual activities, individual or team activities; whether you lead or organise any activities; whether your interests may conflict with or complement the job (eg time commitments, organising ability), and so on.

Many of the following examples can be adapted to cover a wide range of interests.

- What do you do in your spare time?
- Do you have a hobby? What about it interests you most? What advice would you give to someone starting this hobby?
- Do you play any sport?
- How much time do you devote to it?
- How good are you at it?
- What do you get out of it?
- Have you had any particular success with it?
- Have you ever taken a leading or organising role?
- Who is your favourite actor/other practitioner? Why?
- What type of books do you like most? Why?
- What was the last play/other activity you saw/took part in?
- Could you tell me about it?
- How much television do you watch? What type of programmes do you prefer? Why?
- Do you belong to any clubs/societies/voluntary groups?
- What is your social life like?

Ambitions and motivation

This category of question aims to find out what candidates want to do with their lives; what career plans they have (if any); what they enjoy doing; what they get from it; whether their ambitions are realistic; what they want out of a job; what drives them; how much enthusiasm they have for particular activities; what their commitments are to these things; how they feel about their progress; and many other things.

The purpose of this information is to determine candidates' attitudes to work in general and the position on offer in particular. Most of this is obtained indirectly, through their answers to other questions (eg on interests, and the enjoyable/unpleasant aspects of their current job) during the course of the interview. However, there are some more direct questions that may be asked. For example:

- What made you apply for this job?
- What are this organisation's main areas of operation?
- What do you know about our products/services?
- Who is the head of the organisation?
- What parts of the organisation interest you most/least? Why?
- Are you considering any alternatives to this job? Why? What are they?
- If you got this job and were made a better offer within the next six months, would you accept it?
- Would you be willing to move to another region if necessary?
- What do you want out of a job?
- What are you looking for in an employer?
- How would you feel about having to work extra hours?
- What will you do if you do not get this job?
- What would be your next step after this job, if you got it?
- How much fulfilment do you get from work? Is this increasing as your career progresses?
- Do you set yourself objectives (in general, at work)?
- Do you try to improve your performance at work? How?
- Where do you see yourself in five years' time?
- Given the choice, what type of work would you most like to do?

Job and organisation

Many of the questions on this subject also fall into other categories, particularly ambitions and motivation. Candidates' answers can indicate how much interest they have in the job and organisation; how much they know about the position they are applying for; whether they are prepared for what the job entails; and whether they are committed to this type of work and the organisation. Some of these examples have been given in other sections.

- What do you think may be the most/least attractive aspects of this job?
- Is there anything in this job that you wish you had in your current job?
- What are you looking for in an employer?
- What do you think of this organisation?

- How do you rate this company as a place to advance your career?
- What do you know about this organisation/type of work?
- What qualities/skills do you think are required to be successful in this job?

General topics

Questions on general topics such as current affairs, social and other issues, are not often asked, although they do arise, most often in the public sector and at panel interviews.

Candidates' answers to this type of question can reveal things such as whether or not they take an interest in the world at large, whether their opinions and ideas are well founded, and how well they can form and express opinions. Interviewers may, for example, take the opposing viewpoint to see how well candidates can hold their position in a discussion, and whether they are open to other peoples' points of view or fixed in their ideas.

The range of possible topics is enormous, although it can be narrowed down. Interviewers are unlikely to ask questions on 'sensitive' issues, such as aspects of politics, religion, or nationality. The most popular topics are things of current national and international importance in the news; prominent local issues (for the candidate) or those which concern the particular industry or profession; topics related to the job or organisation; topics which candidates have raised during the interview or in application forms; and the interviewers' own interests. It is usually the major issues which are raised, and your research on the job and organisation – together with paying attention to the news media in the days before your interview – should give you a good idea of the most likely topics.

These examples show the *type* of questions that occur most frequently:

- Which daily newspaper do you read? Why that one? Which part do you normally read first? What parts don't you read? What items caught your eye today?
- What do you think of newspapers which publish sensational stories about people's private lives?
- What do you think of the system of education in this country?
- What do you think is wrong with the training provision for young people in this country? How would you improve it?
- If this company ran a private health-care scheme, would you join? Why?
- What measures would you take to protect the environment?

Bosses reveal 'vital' interview questions

by IAN FLETCHER

THREE out of four bosses admit that they try to stump job-seekers with a "killer question" during an interview, a new report reveals today.

Candidates are now being warned that their career prospects may depend on how they cope with the unexpected poser.

It may be "Tell me a joke" or "Would you ever lie in the interests of your job?" But the applicant's response to it could mean the difference between success and failure.

According to the survey by secretarial recruiters Office Angels, bosses insist that these tricky questions are not designed to deliberately catch people out but simply to encourage those in the "hot seat" to show they can think on their feet.

Employers' other favourites include: "What was the question you didn't want me to ask you?", "Give me three things to remember you by", and "Name five members of the Cabinet."

Completing the "killer" top 10 are: "How would I know you were under pressure?", "How have you benefited from your disappointments?", "What kind of people do you find it most difficult to work with?", "What was the last book you read?" and "What do you not have that we need for this job?"

According to the survey, 95 per cent of bosses say they enjoy interviewing. However, 68 per cent claim candidates could be better prepared and show greater enthusiasm.

They identify three key areas where interviewees consistently fail to impress — inappropriate dress (30 per cent), arrogance (27 per cent) and monosyllabic responses (25 per cent).

Some candidates get the simplest things wrong — 48 per cent of employers claim people have arrived late without offering an apology.

But being honest about your concerns regarding a position is looked upon as a plus point.

ds

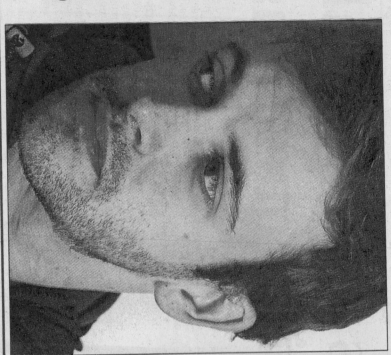

Starspotting: Jonny Lee Miller will present an Evening Standard drama award

- Do you think companies have a responsibility to help protect the environment?

Specialist and technical topics

This type of question is obviously only likely to arise in certain situations, such as in technical and scientific fields. The depth of questioning will depend on the interviewer and the level of knowledge which it can be safely assumed the candidates possess. For example when candidates' qualifications are borderline, the interviewer is more likely to want to 'test' their knowledge and abilities. This type of question also enables the interviewer to assess how well candidates can explain their work to non-technical people (as the interviewer may be), and to find out whether they have thought about how they could apply their expertise in the job.

If you work in one of these areas, you may be required to take a project or some other work to the interview to discuss with the interviewer. If this is the case, at least some of the questions will relate to this material. Otherwise, the questions could be on almost any topic related to your specialism. It is not relevant to give specific examples here, because they vary so much, but the questions will centre around the following types of theme:

- Can you explain that concept to me in a way that a lay person could understand?
- Look at this diagram. Can you explain its meaning to me? What is its significance?
- Can you draw me a simple diagram that would explain that idea?
- What do you think is likely to be the next development in that field?
- Could you explain to me what you consider to be the most significant aspects of your research findings?
- Did you see the paper on 'X' in the 'Y' Journal? What do you think is the significance of their findings?
- If you had the resources, what type of research would you like to undertake? Why?
- Can you explain to me how research is in this area is funded? Do you think the funding is adequate? How much more is needed in your opinion?

Family background and circumstances

Questions on family background are more frequent for young candidates who do not have much work experience. In that situation, their family life still constitutes the major part of their experience and will naturally have been the major influence on their personality, character and general view of life. However, even under these circumstances the subject is not always covered.

One of the reasons for asking about family background is to determine how candidates have done in relation to their domestic environment. For example, how does their performance in examinations rate, bearing in mind that they received no support or encouragement from their parents and the family is in financial hardship? Knowledge of family background and circumstances can also give other information, such as the type of situations candidates are familiar with, the type of people they mix with, and whether domestic circumstances might interfere with the job (eg if it requires periods away from home).

In asking questions on these subjects, there are legal restrictions on the type of questions interviewers can ask if they intend to use that information as a basis for selection. For example, if an interviewer asked a woman if she plans to have a family, because he or she did not want to employ someone who may leave suddenly, it would be illegal. Similarly, questions about ethnic origin, religious beliefs and sexual orientation are unlawful if they are used to obtain information on which to base a selection.

Despite the existence of these laws, interviewers do ask these types of question and they may justify them on the basis that it helps to get a better understanding of the individual. Some questions which interviewers would find it difficult to justify asking have been included in the list below:

- What is your father's job?
- Does your mother work? What does she do?
- Do you have any brothers or sisters? What ages are they? Do they work? What do they do?
- Where do you live?
- How do you get on with your family/individual members?
- When do you plan to leave home? Why at that time?
- What did your parents feel about you staying on/leaving school/ going to college?
- Has any member of your family influenced your choice of career/ subjects at school/college?
- Were you born in this country? When did you move here? Do you intend to stay?

- When did your parents come to this country?
- Do you intend to start a family? When?
- What does your partner think about you applying for this job?
- Do you mind travelling?
- Would your partner mind when you have to be away?
- Do you take a share in managing the household/looking after the children?
- If your partner moved to another region, would you go too?
- Do you have a current driving licence? Do you have any endorsements?
- Do you own a car? What make/model?

Health

It is unusual for interviewers to ask questions about candidates' health. Job offers are often made conditional upon a medical examination, and always when a job requires a high level of physical fitness. However, if an individual has stated a disability or some other incapacity, such as through illness, then the interviewer will naturally need to find out whether this will have any implications for the person's ability to do the job effectively. Anyone in this position will be well aware of the type of questions that could arise, but there are laws prohibiting discrimination on the grounds of certain disabilities or incapacity.

Self-assessment questions

These are some additional self-assessment questions which vary from those given in other categories:

- How would you describe yourself?
- If I asked a friend of yours/your manager/teacher to describe your good/bad qualities, what do you think that person might say?
- What do you see as your strengths/weaknesses?
- Have you ever had doubts about your ability to do something?
- Has anyone ever strongly criticised you? In what way? Was it deserved?
- What qualities do you think you could improve upon?
- What do you see as your most valuable quality?
- What have you got in your favour to advance in this career?
- What about you has helped/hindered your career so far?
- What things motivate you?

- In what area have you developed most in the past three years?
- What do you feel confident/less confident doing?
- What has been the most difficult thing you have had to do in life? Why do you say that?
- What are the major influences that have made you the person you are today?

From the examples given under these various subject headings, you should be aware of the way in which the phrasing of questions can be varied to give them a slightly different meaning. It is impossible to predict how your interviewer will phrase questions, but you should be able to work out from your own circumstances which of the topics listed are most likely to be covered. You can familiarise yourself with the type of questions asked, and practise answering them, when you rehearse (Chapter 9).

As explained in an earlier chapter, the number of questions you will be asked, and how searching they will be, will depend on the type of interview. Chapter 8 helps you to understand what impression different types of answer create and to plan what you want to say in answer to questions.

Key Points

- Interviewers can use questions in different ways to probe until they get the information they need.
- The subject and phrasing of questions enables interviewers to focus on those topics about which they need information.
- You can predict the topics that are most likely to be covered and familiarise yourself with the type of questions that are often asked.

Project 7

This project may take you a while to complete, but it is a very important part of your preparation. It asks you to compile a list of the questions you feel are most likely to be asked in your interview, which you will use for your rehearsal (Chapter 9).

Head separate pieces of paper with the following subject headings: education and training; work history and experience; interests; ambitions and motivation; family background. If it is relevant to you, add specialist and technical matters, and health. Some of these categories will be more important to your situation than others. Now look at the personal profile from Project 3, which lists the characteristics required in the ideal candidate. Write down each of the most important characteristics under each of the question subject headings, leaving at least a third of an A4 page between them. You will probably need several sheets for each heading.

You are now ready to start listing the questions you think are most likely to come up in your interview. Cover each subject heading in turn, looking through the relevant section of this chapter. For each characteristic, list the aspects of the subject which the interviewer could ask you about to find out whether or not you have that characteristic. The most likely topics to arise are going to be those which relate to the information the interviewer already has about you, and that which you will reveal during the interview. For example, if the job requires a strong competitive nature, under the heading 'education and training' you might include examination grades, competitions entered, prizes won, and your involvement in competitive sports or other pastimes at school or college. Do this for all characteristics under all subject headings.

Next, for each item you have listed, write down an example of the type of question that the interviewer could ask on that topic to discover whether or not you have that particular characteristic. This may take some thought at first, but it gets easier. Do this for all the subject headings, and then consider the remaining subject categories.

Self-assessment
The best way to compile a list of self-assessment questions is to follow these steps:

- list what you feel are your good and bad points;
- ask someone else to list what they feel are your good and bad points;
- using the examples given in this chapter, write down some self-assessment questions which would help to reveal these good and bad points.

General topics
Make a list of the *major* issues of the day. It will help if you look through a newspaper such as the *Daily Telegraph, Independent, Guardian*, or *The Times*. When you have done this, translate those topics into questions. There are too many possibilities to cover every question on every issue, so try to get a range of questions like the examples given in this chapter.

Job and organisation

Use the examples in this chapter, and your knowledge of the job and organisation, to compile a list of questions that the interviewer could ask to find out the level of your knowledge about, your interest in, and commitment to, the job and organisation.

Compiling these lists is a time-consuming and laborious task. However, if you treat it as a challenge, you should be able to work up some enthusiasm. And remember, this is an important step in your preparation.

8 ▶ HOW BEST TO ANSWER QUESTIONS

Imagine that you need some detailed information urgently. You ask two people. The first 'ummms' and 'ahhhs', rambles on for a while, hesitates, then gives a slightly different answer, and eventually you get some of the information you need but not all. The second person appears to be reading your thoughts and answers your questions precisely and clearly, telling you all that you wanted to know and even giving you some extra useful information. Which person would create the most favourable impression on you? The interview is a similar situation. By answering questions well, apart from showing that you have the qualities required, you create the impression of being alert, fluent, spontaneous and efficient.

In normal conversation most of us make ourselves understood with ease, reacting spontaneously to any questions we are asked. With a bit of effort we can even impress with the way that we express our ideas and thoughts. However, as soon as we become nervous that natural talent deserts us. We don't listen properly because we are too busy feeling anxious; our minds go blank at crucial moments and, when we do eventually decide what to say, it tends to come out garbled. To get that natural talent working in an interview, and to give it some extra polish, we need to decide beforehand how we are going to express ourselves.

There are three basic steps in answering a question well:

- understanding the question;
- deciding what you want to say; and
- expressing it effectively.

Following each of these steps is vital if you want to answer questions well. You should consider them as completely separate things to achieve for each and every question that you are asked in the interview.

What does the question mean?

Even when people are not very good at expressing themselves it is usually possible for us to understand them, so you may feel that it will be relatively straightforward to understand the meaning of your interviewer's questions. On the surface that may be true, but you must remember that the interviewer is using the questions to help build an impression of you. The questions have a purpose and, if you want to control the impression you create, you must understand the intention behind each question you are asked.

Activity 13

Before reading the guidelines, describe what you think the interviewer's purpose is in the following situations.

1. Remains silent after you have finished giving your answer.
2. Asks, 'Do you think this job will suit you?'
3. Asks, 'Could you explain that to me again?'

Guidelines

What the interviewer was trying to achieve on each of these occasions would depend very much on the situation. For example:

1. If you have given a short, incomplete answer to a question then the interviewer may be encouraging you to continue talking by keeping silent. If, on the other hand, you have given a comprehensive answer, the interviewer is probably taking time to think about your answer and decide what to ask next.
2. This is a closed question, to which you could answer a simple 'yes' or 'no'. But is that the answer the interviewer wants? With this particular question the interviewer is probably asking you to explain how you see yourself fitting into the job – the qualities that make you suitable. However, a question like 'Do you spend much time at the squash club?' when you have been talking for too long on your favourite pastime, would probably be intended to encourage a short answer and stop you talking.

3. If you are asked to explain something again it could mean various things. Perhaps the interviewer didn't understand you because you mumbled or your explanation was muddled or incomplete; or maybe the interviewer was surprised at what you said (eg if you have suggested that you are a very difficult person to work with) and wants to check that you meant what you said.

From these examples it should be clear that the purpose of a question, and therefore its meaning for the candidate, depends on a variety of factors. Not all of these are apparent in the examples, but they include:

- the type of question (eg open-ended, closed);
- the literal meaning of the question;
- the previous and current topic of conversation;
- the interviewer's tone of voice and body language;
- the direction of the conversation;
- what the candidate has said in answer to the previous question(s);
- how the interviewer has responded;
- periods of silence.

The way in which these factors influence the meaning of a question should be apparent from your general experience and from the explanation given in the previous chapter.

It is very important that you understand the meaning of a question before you start to think about your answer. If the question has not been stated clearly, or if you have not heard it properly, then you should ask the interviewer to clarify it. Never try to answer a question which you have not understood. It is perfectly acceptable to say something like, 'I don't quite understand what you mean.'

It is only when you know the true meaning of a question that you can answer it effectively. That means being constantly attentive – listening, watching, and interpreting the interviewer's intentions.

Deciding what to say

Although the interview is not under your control, and you may feel rather intimidated by the interviewer, you have the choice of what you say about yourself and what you do not say. This does not mean that you should lie or try to deceive the interviewer, nor can you avoid answering questions, but you can be selective in most of what you say about yourself. Project 8, together with the following notes, will help you to decide what information to give in your answers to create the most favourable impression. This section deals with some general points and then looks at the individual subjects that may arise in the interview.

At the end of your preparation you should know what information you want to get across. It is unlikely that the interviewer will ask for all of this information and therefore you have to work it into your answers to other questions or make other opportunities to give the information. You will soon get an idea, once the interview has started, of how thoroughly you are going to be questioned. The less thorough the questioning, the more you will have work to introduce your good points.

Open-ended questions (eg Why do you think you are suited to this job?) offer an ideal opportunity to do this. *Closed* questions can also be used to advantage. For example, instead of answering 'no' to the question, 'Were you involved in any team activities at school?', a candidate might say, 'No, but I was group leader on an outward bound course last year.'

Another method is to steer the conversation on to the topic you want to discuss. For example, if you have experience or knowledge in a particular field, you could ask whether there will be an opportunity to use it in the job, explaining that you have enjoyed the experience or would like to apply or develop your knowledge.

When answering *leading questions* (eg You will need to attend a training course once a week; do you mind that?), in general you should give the answer the interviewer is looking for. However, you can still use the opportunity, if appropriate, to say something good about yourself (eg Yes, I'm eager to improve myself). If you are given the opportunity to ask questions at the end of the interview this is another ideal opportunity to introduce your good points.

Obviously you should not volunteer information which is disadvantageous, about your weaknesses or past mistakes for example, although you may be asked to give this type of information, particularly through *self-assessment* questions. However, even then, you can often turn this to advantage (*see page* 91).

Multiple questions can cause some confusion – deciding which part to answer first – but they also offer you an opportunity. You can choose to answer first that part which enables you to put across some of your good points. The chances are that, by the time you have given your answer, the interviewer will be ready to move on to the next question. Alternatively, if you have nothing particularly favourable to say, you can choose that part of the question which you would find easiest to answer. One of the dangers of this approach is that you may appear to be avoiding part of the question. Unless you are going to 'score' some good points it is best to answer each part of the question in turn.

If you are asked how you would deal with a *hypothetical situation* and you are unsure of the best way to answer, you can say something like, 'It's difficult to be precise without being in that situation and having all of the information, but –'. If the interviewer has outlined a problem, you could say, 'I hope that I would have prevented the problem arising but, if it did . . .'. However, if you do this, you may be asked what you would have done to prevent the problem.

One advantage of deciding beforehand what you want to say on particular subjects is that it helps to refresh your memory. Dates and the details of your experience, for example, can be difficult to recall if you have not given them some thought recently. Deciding what information you want to give is basically a matter of common sense – guided by the characteristics required in the ideal candidate – but there are some areas that need careful consideration.

Education and training
If you have not done as well as you would have liked in this area for reasons beyond your control, and choose to explain these, you should be careful that they do not sound like excuses. If you are asked to identify faults in the education or training you have been given, try to make it constructive criticism, perhaps by suggesting how it could have been improved.

Work history and experience
Again, if you are asked for criticism, make it constructive criticism. Be prepared to give your reasons for leaving each of the jobs you have had, particularly why you want to leave your current job in favour of the one on offer. Think about what you will say if you are asked your current or most recent salary. If you refuse to answer this question, and many people do for quite valid reasons, it may be taken to mean that you are currently earning a lot less than is being offered. If you have to explain a long period of unemployment or job hopping, give it very careful consideration. You need to show that unemployment was not self-imposed and that you used the time constructively. If you say that your reason for changing jobs frequently was repeated offers of a better position, it can create a poor impression even if it is true. It suggests that if you get this job, and were subsequently made a better offer, you would not hesitate in leaving. It would be far better to vary the reasons, perhaps including better career opportunities and the chance to gain wider experience.

Interests

Answering questions on this subject is relatively straightforward, but remember that you are trying to highlight your good points and not simply have a friendly chat about what you like to do in your spare time. It is better to state one or two main interests on which you can talk authoritatively, if asked, than to state many just to impress. Don't worry if you feel your main interests might sound boring or give a poor impression. Watching television and going to the pub to play darts are as acceptable as going to the opera or playing the violin. It is how you explain your interest that matters. If you have no interests, be prepared to explain why.

Ambition and motivation

This can be a tricky area. If you are too ambitious you may outgrow the job very quickly, or become dissatisfied. If you lack ambition you may not be interested in improving your performance in the job. Either way it creates a poor impression. You must decide what level of ambition is appropriate for the job. It is good to have some form of career plan, or at least an idea of the direction you want your career to follow in the short term. However, you should not appear to be inflexible or to be setting your sights too high or too low. There is no reason not to say, if asked, that you are applying for other jobs, but you should be prepared to explain the reasons, particularly if the jobs are very different from the one you are being interviewed for.

General topics

The information you need to answer questions on general topics is likely to come from the news media. Newspapers are ideal because you can re-read and study the relevant issues. If your interviewer takes an opposing view to see how well you can defend your viewpoint, you will need a clear understanding of the topic. Your argument should be logical, well founded, and well balanced. If you are asked a question on a topic about which you know very little or nothing, it is best to admit it. Even then you may be asked what you do know.

Specialist and technical topics

It is difficult to prepare for this type of question because they can be so wide-ranging. There are three areas worth concentrating your efforts on: any projects or research you have done; how you could apply your specialist knowledge and skills to the job; areas where your knowledge or skill is weakest.

Family background and circumstances

The only problem you could have in this area is in taking exception to the interviewer's questions because they are intrusive or on the grounds of possible discrimination. It is up to you but, in most circumstances, it is best to answer. If you object very strongly and decide not to answer, be prepared for not being selected. Don't argue the point with the interviewer unless you have decided that you don't want the job anyway. Female candidates asked about their intentions on having children can easily sidestep the issue by saying something like, 'I haven't seriously considered the subject', or, 'No, I don't have any plans to have children in the foreseeable future.' One other point that you should consider seriously is whether, if required, you would be willing to move to a different part of the country.

Health

If there is reason for the interviewer to ask you about your health, you will probably be very well aware of what you want to say in reply to questions. It is very important that anyone with a disability should try not to appear defensive or in any other way 'sensitive' about their situation, because the interviewer may feel this could be a disruptive influence on the job.

Self-assessment

No one is perfect; people who say they are will usually be viewed with suspicion. Admit to your weaknesses, if asked, but try to add some other comment to reduce the impact. For example, if you were asked what qualities you think you could improve upon, it is likely to create a positive impression if, when you identify those qualities, you also say what action you are taking to improve.

If you have prepared for your interview you should be able to start giving your answer to most questions after a few seconds. If you require more thinking time, you can try stalling. You could, for example, get the interviewer to repeat the question by saying that you are not clear what is meant. However, if you do this more than a few times the interviewer will get the impression that you are either not listening or not very bright. If you are asked an unreasonably difficult question, attempt to answer but explain first why you find it difficult. Never try to evade answering a question.

Giving your answers

Apart from the information you give, the way that you structure your answers and speak can say a lot about you. For example, it can reveal whether you think logically and how good you are at communicating face to face. It reflects your personality and can even reveal how truthful you are being.

Activity 14

Imagine someone has decided what information to give in answer to the questions asked in an interview. Draw up a list of guidelines they could follow to help them convey that information effectively to the interviewer. Then read the guidelines below.

Guidelines

When you answer a question you should aim to do the following things:

- keep to the point – aim to be concise but give a full answer;
- structure your answer so that it is logical and can be easily understood;
- avoid using specialist words that the interviewer may not understand;
- make sure you have eye-contact with the interviewer before you start speaking;
- speak up in a confident voice;
- speak clearly, slowing the speed at which you speak if necessary;
- use your voice in a way that reflects the meaning of what you are saying;
- let your posture, facial expressions and gestures be a natural part of what you are saying;
- avoid body language which conflicts with what you are saying;
- don't argue with the interviewer unless you are being encouraged to defend your viewpoint. Even then, remain agreeable.

While you are giving your answer, and when you finish, you should be watching for the way the interviewer reacts. This can be useful in telling you things such as whether or not you are giving the right information, and whether you need to qualify or explain something you have said – perhaps because the interviewer doesn't seem to understand or is surprised at what you have said. Facial expressions are a good indicator of the interviewer's reaction.

An interviewer's apparent reaction or general behaviour can also worry or confuse candidates. If the interviewer looks away or sounds uninterested, as if bored, or writes something down while the candidate is talking, as if it is something incriminating, it can be unsettling. You must be aware of the interviewer's reactions to what you are saying so that you can respond appropriately, but the only time this should give you cause for concern is when you are failing to present yourself well – which should not arise if you have prepared properly.

When you stop speaking the interviewer may indicate that you should continue, perhaps with a word or phrase such as 'Yes', or 'I see', which sounds expectant, or by looking you in the eye and saying nothing. If you have prepared properly, and think you have given as good (complete, clear) an answer as possible, you should resist the temptation to say more. If you continue you risk creating a poor impression by rambling on just for the sake of it.

If the interviewer says something which shows that what you said has been misunderstood, it is important that you make this clear straight away by saying something like, 'No, I'm sorry, I don't think you understand what I meant.' You are unlikely to get another opportunity to do this; even if you do, the interviewer will already have absorbed the earlier, inaccurate meaning.

Your final opportunity for giving any information which you have not yet been able to get across comes near the end of the interview. If the interviewer asks if you have any questions (or if you ask), it is often possible to raise a question which enables you to say something about yourself at the same time. An example might be, 'Yes, perhaps you could tell me if there are any opportunities for doing statistical work, because I have some experience of that and I find it very interesting.' Another way of introducing this information is to say something like, 'One thing that I haven't mentioned, that you may feel is relevant, is that …'. Obviously, you can only do this with information which is directly relevant and which is important enough to raise at this late stage.

This chapter should have given a clear idea of what type of thing to say in answer to questions, and how best to say it. To make sure that you can put theory into practice it is necessary to rehearse, which is the subject of Chapter 9.

Key Points

● The first step in answering a question well is to make sure that you understand the meaning of the question; this involves being constantly attentive – listening, watching, and interpreting what the interviewer is trying to achieve.

● When you know what a question means you can decide what information to give about yourself to create a favourable impression; all of this should be familiar from your preparation and it is simply a matter of recalling what is appropriate to the question.

● When you give your answer it should be clear, concise, easily understood and sound natural.

Project 8

This project asks you to identify what you want to reveal about yourself in the interview. You will use these notes when you rehearse (Chapter 9).

Look at your notes from Project 7. Start with the subject headings and work through each one in turn. For each topic under each characteristic, list the positive things you could say about yourself. It is very unlikely that you will have something positive to say in every case. In those situations, try to think of something else you could say on a related topic under any subject heading. If, during the interview, you are asked a question which is obviously looking for evidence of your ability in a particular area, often you will be able to change the topic of conversation (eg from current job to leisure interests) in order to show that you have that ability. Repeat this process and note all the things that you do *not* want to say – those which create a less than favourable impression.

When you have covered all the subject headings, look at the self-assessment questions you listed. Some of these prompt you to reveal negative information about yourself. Try to think of what else you can say to reduce the impact of that information, and even turn it to advantage.

For questions on the job and organisation you should already have all the information you need from Project 5. For questions on general topics it is not worthwhile deciding what you want to say, because you cannot predict what topics might arise. However, you can rehearse answering this type of question. As part of this project, collect some newspaper cuttings on at least a dozen major current issues on which you can answer questions during rehearsal.

9 ▶ PRACTISING FOR YOUR INTERVIEW

It is all very well reading about what you should do in your interview, but it is not necessarily easy to put that into practice on the day. This chapter will help you to rehearse your interview performance, based on the preparation you have done reading through the previous chapters.

It takes some effort to read a book, a bit more to do the exercises in this book, and a lot of effort to rehearse. However, once you have made the effort and got started, you will soon realise how beneficial it is to have a practice run.

The reasons for rehearsing

Being interviewed is not like taking part in a normal conversation where, even if you have planned what you want to say, you usually feel quite relaxed in responding spontaneously to the flow of the conversation. You may know exactly how you want to behave and respond in your interview but because it is a stressful situation, and relatively uncommon to most people, it is difficult to feel relaxed or confident enough to behave normally.

Rehearsal for an interview is mostly about building confidence. It is also about becoming familiar with expressing yourself effectively in an interview situation, and getting across the information that makes you a suitable candidate for selection.

Activity 15

Bearing in mind the purpose of rehearsing for your interview, briefly describe how you would go about it. Then read on.

Guidelines

You need three things for a rehearsal – an understanding of how to rehearse, a knowledge of what to rehearse, and someone to take the role of the interviewer and give you feedback on your performance.

Methods of rehearsing

A number of schools and colleges run courses designed to give students practice in presenting themselves at interviews and offer expert guidance on their performance. Video or audio tape playback is often used to help individuals improve their performance. Even if you do not have access to such a course, and are still at school or college, you could ask the careers adviser or a member of the teaching staff if it would be possible to organise practice sessions. Another way of getting practice is by going for interviews – though then you only have your own opinion of your performance instead of feedback and guidance from someone else.

If you do not have access to a properly organised course you can, with the cooperation of another person (or several if you are rehearsing for a panel interview), use this chapter to run your own practice sessions. The person you choose to help you will often depend on who is available and willing to help. Ideally it should be someone that you do not know too well (as your interviewer will be), and who has experience of interviews (and being successful at them!). However, you may not have a choice. It could be someone leaving school or college at the same time as you, a careers adviser or teacher, a colleague at work, a friend or parent.

When you have found someone willing to help you, ask that person to read this chapter to gain an idea of what it will involve.

What to rehearse

The exact content of your rehearsal will depend upon the purpose of your interview, but it should cover every aspect of communicating information to the interviewer. This includes:

- your answers to all the questions you could be asked, as well as handling unexpected questions;

- your voice;
- your body language, facial expressions, and eye-contact;
- your attitude and manner;
- asking questions.

In addition, you can also practise using relaxation exercises. Since you will not need any help with these, they are dealt with towards the end of this chapter.

How to rehearse

If possible, find a setting for your rehearsal which is close to that which you can expect in your interview. Give the person helping you the job description you prepared in Project 3 and the list of questions from Project 7. This provides background information and questions to ask you. Ask your helper to vary the wording of these questions and to ask additional questions, related to the job, for which you will be unprepared. Conduct the rehearsal as if it were the real thing, going through all the stages that were outlined in Chapter 5, starting with you entering the interview room. Explain to your helper what this involves.

It is best to have several rehearsals and, if possible, to use a tape recorder or even video camera to record your performance. This will enable you to relate your performance to the feedback you get from your helper. At first you should use your notes from Project 8 to help you recall the information you want to give in answer to the questions. In later rehearsals you should begin to do this from memory until you no longer need prompting. Your helper should use the checklist given later to assess your performance. (You may need to explain how to recognise some of the things listed.) Then, in between rehearsals, you may want to look back through earlier chapters of this book for guidance on how to improve your performance.

It is not a good idea to try to become word perfect in answering questions. Firstly, the interviewer may phrase the questions in a slightly different way and you could quite easily miss the difference and give an inappropriate answer. For example, instead of asking 'How do you think you would get on with the other people in the department?', the interviewer may say, 'What do you think you might gain from working with the other people in the department?' Secondly, it is much easier to answer questions spontaneously than to remember word for word what you want to say. Your answers will also sound spontaneous, which will create a better impression.

However, there are some situations in which you may want to think about how you would word what you say. In describing something technical to a non-technical interviewer, for example, you would need to avoid jargon and make your explanation easy for a lay person to understand. You can try out your wording of this type of comment during your rehearsal.

Assessing your performance

The following checklist is for your helper to use in assessing your performance during rehearsals. You could also use it, although not as effectively, to assess your own performance. You can add additional points to this list, such as specific things which you find difficult to do when you are nervous. It is a good idea to include points which reflect the characteristics required in the ideal applicant, if they are not covered here, as well as their opposites. Once you have updated the list make copies, one for each of your practice sessions.

UNDERLINE THE APPROPRIATE WORD OR PHRASE:

Answers to questions:

Clear/unclear	Words chosen well/poorly
Well structured/muddled	Easy/difficult to follow
Comprehensive/insufficient	Rambling
Irrelevant information	Hesitant/confident
Quick/slow to respond	Rash/thoughtful

The voice:

Confident/nervous	Natural/forced
Clear/mumbled	Quiet/loud/right level
Fast/slow/natural speed	Enthusiastic/uninterested
Rich/meaningful	Dull/uninteresting

Posture:

Upright/slouched	Relaxed/tense/nervous
Attentive/uninterested	Confident/uncertain

Gestures:

Too expansive/restricted   Natural/nervous

Distracting   Fidgeting

Facial expressions:

Natural/forced   Responsive/unresponsive

Enthusiastic/uninterested   Lifeless/animated

Nervous/relaxed   Conflicting with words

Eye-contact:

Normal/staring/avoiding   Distracted/attentive

Attitude and manner:

Sincere/insincere   Convincing/unconvincing

Relaxed/nervous   Agreeable/irritating

Confident/overconfident   Lacks confidence

Enthusiastic/uninterested   Quiet/outspoken

Assertive/passive   Natural/forced

Serious/flippant/pleasant   Argumentative/controlled

Involved/distant   Rash/thoughtful

Questions asked:

Rash/thoughtful   Intelligent/irrelevant

Well structured/muddled   Words chosen well/poorly

Knowledgeable   Too demanding

Hesitant/confident   Rambling

Shows interest/lack of interest

NOTE: This assessment can be made and amended during and/or immediately after the practice session.

Improving your performance

When you get feedback from your helper, don't be too dismayed if it doesn't look encouraging. Without some critical comments you would have little idea of where your performance could be improved. Spend some time with your helper going through the checklist, looking at each item in turn and discussing how you performed in each area. Note your strengths and weaknesses and make some notes on how you could overcome those weaknesses.

You may simply need more practice, or to refer to earlier chapters, or perhaps to revise your notes from Project 8. When you feel you know how you can do better, have another practice run. Repeat this process until you are confident that you are presenting yourself in the best possible way. A checklist is provided later to help you assess how well you are prepared.

If you have to wait for your helper to be available again, you can practise some things by yourself. For example, you can think through all the varieties of questions that you could be asked and how you would answer them; you can practise speaking your answers aloud, perhaps making a recording on audio tape to listen to how well you convey meaning and emotion; and you can use a mirror to note the image you create through your posture, gestures and facial expressions. It is also a good idea to try on the clothes you will wear, to make sure that they look good and that you feel comfortable in them.

It may take five or more rehearsals before you feel confident, but remember that on the day you will probably feel more nervous that you do in practice, so it is important to feel happy with your performance at this stage.

Controlling interview nerves

Signs of nervousness – like trembling and sweaty palms – indicate that the body is energised for action. The body naturally produces adrenalin in tense situations or when we are excited or frightened. The difference between fear and excitement is in our mind and has nothing to do with how we feel physically.

We can turn this build-up of adrenalin accompanying nervousness to our advantage. This involves distracting ourself from the situation which is making us nervous, and channelling the energy into something useful like enthusiasm. It is useful to relax before going in for the interview. This can be done, inconspicuously, by sitting in a chair and letting your arms hang down loosely by your sides. Then close your eyes and concentrate on your breathing. This exercise can help you to stop worrying about what is about to happen. If you practise relaxation regularly, it will be easier to remain calm on the day.

How well prepared are you?

You should rehearse (including practising relaxation) until you are confident that you can create the best possible impression in your interview. Answer the following questions to judge how well you are prepared.

- Do you feel confident that you could answer almost any question the interviewer might ask?
- Could you handle unexpected questions without getting flustered?
- Despite interview nerves, are you confident that you will be able to
  - think clearly?
  - structure your answers clearly?
  - speak clearly?
- Are you clear about the image you want to project?
- Can you project that image convincingly through
  - what you say (and don't say)?
  - your voice?
        posture?
        gestures?
        eye-contact?
        facial expressions?
        manner and attitude?
  - the questions you ask?
  - the way you dress?
- Do you know a relaxation exercise that works well for you, which you could use before your interview?

If you answered 'no', or a doubtful 'yes', to any of these questions, you could probably do with some more practice. When the day of your interview arrives you should be fully rehearsed. It is unwise to rehearse on the day of your interview because it can be worrying if, for some reason, it does not go well. Project 9 gives some suggestions on what you can do the evening before, and on the day of your interview. Chapter 10 provides a checklist for you to use after the interview to assess your performance.

Key Points

- Rehearsing your interview helps you to practise projecting a positive image and builds your confidence.
- It is important to rehearse all the ways in which you communicate information about yourself to the interviewer.
- You should rehearse until you are confident that you can create the best possible image.

Project 9

In order to make full use of the preparation you have done you need to feel alert, relaxed and confident during your interview. These simple suggestions are intended to help you.

A. *The evening before your interview:*

1. Don't drink too much alcohol, even though you may feel that the effects will have worn off by the time of your interview.
2. Try to get a good night's sleep.

The after-effects of alcohol and lack of sleep can make you less alert and leave you feeling less able to cope with the challenge that your interview presents.

B. *On the day of your interview:*

1. Set out on time.
2. Try the following exercises, perhaps while travelling:

    (a) Imagine that you have asked someone who knows you well to tell you all of your good qualities. Think of all the things they may say.
    (b) Try to recall all that you have done really well.
    (c) Think about the type of people you would like to work with, and the type of work and working environment you would most enjoy.
    (d) Practise ways of relaxing and use these within an hour of your interview starting.

(a) and (b) can help to boost your confidence; (c) acts as a reminder that you are not the only one being interviewed – what if the job or the organisation doesn't meet your requirements?; (d) is self-explanatory.

10 ▶ AFTER YOUR INTERVIEW – WHAT NEXT?

We all learn from experience and this is most effective when we analyse what we have done and identify how we could have performed better. This chapter is designed to help you to:

- think about what happened in your interview;
- assess how well you presented yourself;
- identify areas where you could improve;
- take appropriate action to improve.

Analysing your interview performance

To improve the way you do something you first need to consider all that it involves; then you identify those areas where you could perform better. You should do the next activity as soon as possible after your interview – ideally, within 24 hours. It is important to do this as soon as possible after the interview because you can forget the details of what happened, and your impressions of it can change.

 Activity 16

Answer all the following questions. They are designed to ensure that you cover all aspects of your performance.

1. How well do you feel you presented yourself in the interview?
2. What was the experience of being interviewed like (eg enjoyable, frightening, interesting)? Why?

3. How was the interview conducted? (List the sequence of events, and say whether you feel it was done effectively.)
4. What questions were you asked? (List as many as you can recall.)
5. Which of these had you anticipated, and which were unexpected?
6. What was your impression of the interviewer (eg pleasant, friendly, threatening, formal, superior)?
7. Which questions did you answer well/poorly? How did you answer them and why did you do so in this way?
8. Did you give any answers that you now think you could have made clearer or more complete?
9. Could your answers have been more effective in creating a favourable impression? How?
10. Did you feel uncertain about what to say in response to any questions? Why?
11. Did you ramble at any time?
12. Did you manage to convey all the information you wanted to about yourself?
13. Did you say anything that you now regret having said?
14. Were you always aware of the interviewer's reactions? Did you respond appropriately?
15. Do you think you appeared relaxed and confident throughout the interview?
16. Did nervousness hinder your performance in the interview?
17. Did you show that you were interested in the job (eg through your knowledge of the organisation, and your enthusiasm)?
18. Throughout the interview, did you look alert, attentive, and pleased to be there?
19. What sort of impression do you think you made on greeting the interviewer?
20. Had this impression changed by the end of the interview? If so, how did it change, and why?
21. Did you say or do anything which you think the interviewer disapproved of? If so, what? What do you think was the reason for the disapproval?
22. Overall, do you think you successfully conveyed the impression you wanted to give?
23. Besides questions, did anything happen for which you were unprepared? How did you cope?
24. Did you ask any questions? (If you did, list them.)
25. Were your questions relevant/intelligent? What impression do you think they created?

26. Did you get all the information you wanted from the interviewer? If not, why not?
27. Overall, do you think you were well prepared?
28. Do you think you could have done better with more practice?
29. If you could do the interview again, what would you change and why?

Guidelines

If you have done this activity soon after your interview your answers should give you an accurate impression of your performance and suggest areas where you could improve. For example:

1. Your answer to this question may have changed as you answered subsequent questions. It illustrates the importance of analysing your performance in order to improve.
2. Your attitude to, and feelings about, the interview have an important influence on your performance. For example, if you found it enjoyable because you did not take it seriously, or found it frightening because you did not know what to expect, this suggests areas for improvement.
3. If you feel the interview was not conducted effectively, is there anything you could have done to help the interviewer and, in turn, yourself?
9. Your reasons for feeling uncertain about how to reply to a question may imply that you did not understand the question or had not anticipated it (Were you listening? Should you have asked for clarification? Did you know why the question was asked? Did you know what information was required?).
12. If you regret having said something, this suggests that, at least momentarily, you were not in control. There are many reasons for this happening – nervousness, lack of preparation, or being lulled into a false sense of security by the friendliness of the interviewer.
18 and 19. If the impression you gave the interviewer changed during the interview it indicates that you were not consistent in the way you presented yourself. Any change in the way you present yourself can harm your chances of success as the interviewer will have difficulty in assessing you.

If you analyse your answers you can identify your weaknesses and endeavour to improve your performance.

How to improve your interview performance

Performance at your interview is the result of two separate elements – the planning, preparation and rehearsal you did before the interview, and your performance on the day. It is important to make this distinction because you need to identify where you must make changes. For example, the reason for not answering a question effectively could be not hearing the question; failure to anticipate it and prepare an answer; or an inability to recall what you wanted to say or express it clearly. Each of these requires a different solution. You may need to take more care in anticipating likely questions, in preparing or rehearsing your answers, or controlling nervousness.

A careful analysis of your performance will give you a clear idea of how you could improve at your next interview. Looking through the relevant chapters of this book again, as soon as you have completed your analysis, will help you to identify what you need to do differently or more thoroughly in preparing for your interview.

To improve your performance in anything it is important to maintain your strengths as well as overcoming your weaknesses. So, in addition to paying attention to those areas where you could present yourself more effectively, you must not neglect those things which you did well. You need the same careful planning, preparation and rehearsal to maintain your strengths as you do to overcome your weaknesses.

Project 10 asks you to plan what you will do to improve your performance at your next interview.

If you are not successful

Almost everyone, at some time in their lives, is unsuccessful at an interview. If you know that you have done everything you can do to present yourself effectively you should not take rejection personally. It is only fair that someone with a better mix of the qualities required, or better formal qualifications, should be given preference. If you have made an effort to present yourself well, you should not feel any shame or guilt. It may be small comfort, but it is worthwhile bearing in mind some of the other reasons why people are rejected:

- the organisation may, at this time, have a selection policy which excludes certain people (eg it may be anxious to recruit from the minorities, or to change the balance of men/women recruits, or to recruit people with a particular background, or to give preference to graduates);

- the selection criteria may be unreasonably tough (it is not unusual for organisations to have to re-advertise jobs and sometimes settle for less than they originally wanted);
- most people have personal biases, and interviewers are no exception – these can have an unreasonable influence on the final selection;
- the interview can go badly for reasons beyond the candidate's control;
- the organisation may not be good at selection;
- candidates are sometimes rejected because they are 'over-qualified'; or
- competition may be particularly high in the field you have chosen.

One final factor deserves consideration, and that is whether you are the right sort of person for the situation on offer. Many people apply for situations which do not match their personal qualities, or their needs. Some are successful, others are not. Those who are successful may, in the course of time, realise that they have made a mistake and change jobs, or they may develop new qualities and adapt to the situation. However, those who are repeatedly unsuccessful often get disheartened and lose their sense of self-worth.

Whatever your situation, it is important that you decide what it is you want to do with your professional life, both in the short term and the long term. There are increasing numbers of opportunities for you to gain the knowledge, skills and experience that you may require to get on the first rung of the career ladder, or to change career direction. Unless you are clear at the outset what you want, those opportunities will pass you by. You run the risk of never achieving what you would like, and of misdirecting your natural talent and enthusiasm. If you are unsure of the career path you want to follow, and the training and other opportunities available, you should get expert advice. Details of where you can get this type of advice are given at the end of this book.

The future

Whether or not you are successful at this interview, you will most likely attend other interviews in the future, either for promotion or when changing jobs. All interviews give you the chance to practise presenting yourself well, and you should make the most of this opportunity. The more skilled you become at handling interviews the more you will look forward to this means of advancing your chosen career.

In reading this book you may have felt that it is too much effort to plan and prepare for an interview. It does take time and effort but it is worthwhile, if only because you will know that you have given it your best shot. You may also feel that preparing in this way is unnatural, and all you need to do is to be yourself in an interview. In fact, what you are doing is learning to be yourself by overcoming the barriers to communication which occur in the unnatural situation of the interview.

Key Points

- If you analyse your interview performance soon after the event you will be able to identify areas where you could improve.
- When you plan how to improve your performance you should bear in mind that it is important to think about how you can continue to excel at the things you did well.
- If you are unsuccessful at an interview, do not take it personally; on the positive side, it has given you a chance to practise your skills which will be valuable whenever you are interviewed in the future.
- If you have a short or long term career plan, interviews, together with appropriate training if required, are an opportunity for you to achieve what you want in your professional life.

Project 10

Even if you are successful at this interview, spend some time thinking about how you will improve your planning, preparation, rehearsal and presentation for the next one. Make a list of what you will do to maintain the better aspects of your performance in this interview and to overcome your weaknesses.

FURTHER READING & OTHER SOURCES

This is a selection of the sources of information and advice available on interviews and careers opportunities. Details of other sources are given in some of the items listed.

Publications

Ball, Ben. *Manage Your Own Career. A Self-Help Guide to Career Choice & Change*. Kogan Page, London, 1989. Helps readers to identify their interests, skills and values and to explore the jobs market. Twelve questionnaires help readers build up a personal and career profile.

Bramham, John and Cox, David. *Job Hunting Made Easy. A Step-by-Step Guide*. Kogan Page, London, 1987. Includes advice on finding the opportunities; preparing a good application; preparing for the interview; tips on working life; going back to work.

Burston, Diane, ed. *An A–Z of Careers and Jobs*. Kogan Page, London, 1988. Covers more than 350 jobs and careers, listing qualifications and training; personal qualities needed; starting salaries; sources of further advice and information.

Courtis, John. *Selling Yourself in the Management Market*. Kogan Page, London, 1988. Puts the emphasis on getting the *right* job.

Donald, Vivien. *How to Choose a Career*. Kogan Page, London, 1989.

Fletcher, Clive. *How to Face the Interview – and other selection procedures*. Unwin Paperbacks, London, 1986. Includes advice on curriculum vitae, application form, references, letter of application, the interview.

Golzen, Godfrey and Plumbley, Philip. *Changing Your Job After 35*. Sixth edition. Kogan Page, London, 1988.

Gratus, Jack. *Successful Interviewing: how to find and keep the best people.* Penguin, Harmondsworth, 1988. Guidance for interviewers.

Korving, Margaret. *Make a Fresh Start: A Careers Guide for Adults.* Kogan Page, London, 1988. Gives advice on changing jobs and careers.

Miller, Ruth. *Equal Opportunities.* Careers Guide for Men and Women. Penguin, Harmondsworth, 1987.

Occupations 89. The Annual Guide to Opportunities and Trends in Employment. MSC & Careers and Occupational Information Centre.

Parsons, Edward J. *How to Win at the Job Game. A Guide for Executives.* Kogan Page, London, 1985.

Peel, Malcolm. *Readymade Interview Questions.* Kogan Page, London, 1988. Guidance for the interviewer.

Taylor, Felicity. *After School. A Guide to Post School Opportunities.* Kogan Page, London, 1987. Where to find information and advice when deciding what to do next.

Wallis, Margaret. *Getting There: Jobhunting for Women.* Kogan Page, London, 1987.

Yate, Martin John. *Great Answers to Tough Interview Questions. How to Get the Job You Want.* Second edition. Kogan Page, London, 1988.

Kogan Page Careers Series. Practical guides for school-leavers and graduates. Each title covers: careers openings and prospects; educational requirements and training opportunities; how to apply for jobs; university, polytechnic and college courses; likely working conditions.

Kogan Page Guides to Careers. Each titles covers job opportunities; entry requirements; finding work; personal qualities.

Kogan Page Jobs In ... series. Each title covers finding a job; how to apply; training and education; working conditions and salaries; case studies; useful addresses.

Other Sources

Main *reference libraries* usually hold a diverse range of useful information, including providers of education and training, careers opportunities, and commercial information on major employers.

Students in further and higher education have access to a *careers adviser*.

Local authorities provide free careers advice through *careers officers* for anyone up to the age of 19. Some careers officers will see people over this age, although they have no obligation, or will suggest alternative sources of advice. Addresses can usually be found in the telephone directory under 'Careers Service'.

Educational Guidance Shops provide advice and information on courses. Not all local authorities provide this service. Look in your local telephone directory or ask the careers officer.

Organisations that represent your chosen profession or industry can often provide information and advice on careers opportunities and training. Addresses can be found in *Equal Opportunities* (Miller) and *Occupations 89*, both of which should be available at your reference library.

There are companies which provide *private vocational counselling*, for which they charge a fee. Names and addresses can usually be found in the telephone directory under 'careers'.